NEBRASKA

Here is the story of a prairie state where Arbor Day began, where a National Forest was established without a tree in it. Now there is a forest of 22,000 acres of trees, all planted by man.

This land in the heart of a continent was once covered by ancient seas. It is rich in skeletons of prehistoric fish and animals which the Indians called "stone bones."

Oldest human group known to the region were called "Folsom People," who hunted the mammoth.

For years it was a remote land. The first wagon crossed it two hundred years after the Pilgrims landed at Plymouth. Here are the stories of the Oregon Trail that followed the Platte and of Lewis and Clark on the Missouri. Hardy settlers, plagued by grasshoppers and prairie fires, endured twenty-five years of terror from the Indians.

This is the vivid story of the people who made this land their home and built a great state on its fertile soil which is "floating" on a sea of underground water, one of its richest resources. If all this water could be brought up it could cover the state to a depth of 34 feet.

Enchantment of America
NEBRASKA

By Allan Carpenter

Illustrations by Roger Herrington

Ф CHILDRENS PRESS, Chicago

Consultant

Robert N. Manley, Professor of History
The Hiram Scott College, Scottsbluff, Nebraska

For their advice, counsel and gracious help the author thanks:

Frank B. Morrison, Governor
Robert N. Manley, Professor of History, The Hiram Scott College
John E. Lynch, Executive Secretary, Nebraska State Education Association
Nebraskaland, Game, Forestation and Parks Commission, Lincoln
Dick Schaffer, Editor, *Nebraskaland* Magazine
Committee for National Arbor Day, West Orange, New Jersey
Hal Gildersleeve, University of Nebraska Libraries
Omaha Chamber of Commerce
Tom Balow
Public Library, Evanston, Illinois

Library of Congress Catalog Card Number: AC 67-10280

Contents

A True Story to Set the Scene

His Monuments Grow Everywhere

He had been looking forward to joining the people of Nebraska in the first celebration of its kind ever held; he had, in fact, invented and proposed the celebration and through his persuasion it had been made official. Yet when the day finally came, the much disappointed founder of the celebration was not able to take part in it.

The story of that first celebration, of the planning that went before it and of the extraordinary success it had in later years is one of the most interesting stories of the enchantment of Nebraska. It is, as well, a story in which almost everyone now living in the United States has had a part.

Julius Sterling Morton had come to Nebraska in 1855 to take up a home site on a bluff of the Missouri River near newly established Nebraska City. The timber along the river did not extend to his acres, so he began at once to plant shade and fruit trees. As his trees grew, Morton also grew in prominence in the Nebraska region, and he grew more and more convinced that the planting of trees would be one of the greatest blessings for future generations in Nebraska.

In one of his speeches Morton said, "If I had the power, I would compel every man in the State who had a home of his own to plant out and cultivate fruit trees."

This must have given him an idea, for in January, 1872, he presented the following resolution to the State Board of Agriculture: "Resolved, That Wednesday, the 10th day of April, 1872, be, and the same is hereby, especially set apart and consecrated for tree planting in the state of Nebraska, and the State Board of Agriculture hereby name it Arbor Day; and to urge upon the people of the State the vital importance of tree planting, hereby offer a special premium of one hundred dollars to the agricultural society of the county in Nebraska which shall, upon that day, plant properly the largest number of trees; and a farm library of twenty-five dollars' worth of books to that person who, on that day, shall plant properly, in Nebraska, the greatest number of trees."

Although some of the Board thought the name should be "Sylvan Day," they passed the resolution just as it was written. Some authorities feel that Morton's invention of the term Arbor Day was one of the main reasons for its success.

Indeed, even on that first Arbor Day ever celebrated there was a fantastic success. About a million trees were planted in the state that day. Ironically, the founder of Arbor Day, J. Sterling Morton, was not able to take part in the celebration. He had ordered 800 trees for a tree-planting celebration on Arbor Day, then had to suffer through the disappointment of not having them arrive for the day. However, he wrote, "They will come soon and then I will put them out." He had put out thousands before and also planted many more thousands afterward.

On that first Arbor Day, Morton had written to an Omaha newspaper, "Trees grow in time. The poorest landowner in Nebraska has just as large a fortune of time secured to him as has the richest. And the rain and sunshine and seasons will be his partners, just as genially and gently as they will be those of any millionaire, and will make the trees planted by the poor man grow just as grandly and beautifully as those planted by the opulent. . . .

"The wealthiest and most powerful potentate on earth cannot hire one to speed its growth or bear fruit before its time . . . There is a true triumph in the unswerving integrity and genuine democracy of trees . . . Then what infinite beauty and loveliness we can add to the pleasant plains of Nebraska by planting forest and fruit trees upon every swell of their voluptuous undulations, and in another short decade, make her the Orchard of the Union, the Sylvan queen of the Republic. . . ."

Morton's interest in trees was a very practical one. They were needed for fuel, lumber, fencing and many other purposes. Also he felt, as did many others, that forests would hold the rainfall and make the waste places blossom.

Two years after the first Arbor Day, Morton wrote in his diary: "Arbor Day, an invention of mine, now become a public holiday, destined to become a blessing to posterity as well as to ourselves . . . Other holidays repose upon the past; Arbor Day proposes for the future." He could hardly have realized how extraordinarily his day would succeed over the years.

Arbor Day has grown into a holiday celebrated by every state ex-

cept Alaska. Almost every schoolboy and girl in the United States has had a part in the planting of trees on the day that Mr. Morton founded, and for the first time many of them have been made to realize how tremendously important trees are, not only for use and beauty but also for holding our very land itself together.

The success of this worthy movement is a tribute not only to its founder but also to his state of Nebraska which had the faith in him to begin what has been called "America's loveliest custom."

Lay of the Land

Beeline for the Border

The great Paul Bunyan had failed miserably to make a straight border for southern Nebraska. He tried to plow a straight line with his blue ox Babe, but the furrow was very crooked and soon it filled up to become the Republican River. However, Nebraska's own great folk hero, Febold Feboldson, was equal to the task. For this purpose alone, he devoted 15 years of his life to crossing eagles with bees. At last he had great humming insects as large as the noblest eagle. After some difficulty in making harnesses for them, he finally hitched a couple of the strongest "beeagles" to a plow, and they made a perfect beeline across the country. This according to the colorful legend is how the southern Nebraska boundary was formed.

Whatever their origin, all of Nebraska's boundaries are perfectly straight artificial borders except for the Missouri River line on the east and northeast. Nebraska shares the Missouri River with Missouri, Iowa and South Dakota. Other neighbors are Wyoming, Colorado and Kansas.

From its highest point about a mile high in Banner County in the west, Nebraska gently tilts to the east and southeast toward its lowest point in Richardson County, 825 feet above sea level. About half of the state's surface is made up of what is known as Dissected (eroded) Till Plains; the rest is made up of "constructional plains," which are not yet much cut up by erosion.

Twenty counties in north-central Nebraska are included in what is known as the Sandhills area. This once was the bed of a vast, sandy sea; then it was laid bare to wind and water. Over the eons the sand blew into rolling hills and ridges, constantly changing form. In a very recent period, which some say was within the time of European exploration, lush grasses began to grow over the sand. Today the rolling slopes are covered with grasses that hold the sand in place so that except in a few bare spots the sand no longer changes as the winds blow. These almost endless grasslands are said to be different from any other region of the world.

In the west the flowing plains rise abruptly to merge with the Wildcat Hills. Western bluffs and buttes played a leading part as landmarks for travelers in the western movement of peoples. Another outstanding natural Nebraska feature is the Badlands region, an extension of the Badlands of South Dakota.

Waters—Flowing and Landlocked

Nebraska takes its name from the natural feature which dominates it more than any other—the fantastic Platte River. The Omaha Indians called the Platte *Nibathaska;* the Otoe Indians named it *Nibrathka;* both of these words mean "flat, or shallow, water." So Nebraska is literally the land of the flat water. Explorer John C. Frémont said, "The names given by the Indians are always remarkably appropriate; and certainly none was ever more so than that which they have given to this stream—the Nebraska, or Shallow River!"

Near the city of North Platte, the Platte River is formed by the coming together of the North Branch flowing from Wyoming and the South Branch, flowing from Colorado. The Platte is so broad and so shallow in most places that it has been the subject of many joking comments. Humorist Artemus Ward visited the region and said that the Platte would be a good river if set on edge. It has been nicknamed "The Mile-Wide and Inch-Deep."

About three-fourths of Nebraska is drained by the Platte and its tributaries, sometimes flowing as raging torrents due to spring thaws or rains, and other times running almost dry. The Loup River is the largest tributary of the Platte. Others are the Elkhorn, Cedar, Dismal and Calamus.

One of the strange facts about the Platte is that no major tributaries flow into it from the south. This, of course, was why the Oregon Trail was so easy to follow in Nebraska. The Trail followed a "ridge" separating the Platte and Big Blue, so that there was a minimum of rivers to be crossed. The Big Blue River begins only about two miles from the Platte, but instead of flowing into the nearby river, the Big Blue flows north and east and then south to leave the southern boundary of the state; its tributaries the West Fork and the Little Blue also have their beginnings not far from the Platte.

The Republican River flows along much of the southern boundary of Nebraska before leaving the state near Superior. In the north, the

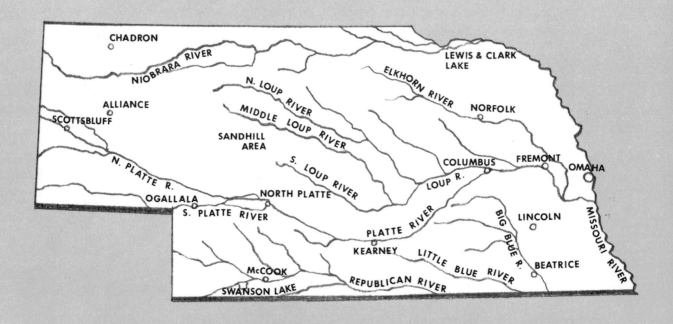

Niobrara River flows almost the entire length of the state until it flows into the Missouri, which, of course, is the most famed river touching Nebraska.

Altogether, there are about 5,765 miles of running water in the state.

Major lakes in the number of 3,350 and innumerable ponds dot the Nebraska landscape. In the Sandhills area alone there are about 2,000 shallow lakes. Largest of the state's lakes is McConaughy, formed by Kingsley Dam, the second largest earthen dam in the world. There are 17 other major man-made lakes in Nebraska. On the Missouri River, popular Lewis and Clark Lake is formed by Gavins Point Dam. It is the only one of the great man-made Missouri River lakes that touches Nebraska. Other lakes and reservoirs of the state include Hugh Butler (Red Willow), Box Butte, Willow, Sherman, Sutherland, Jeffrey, Enders, Swanson, Harlan County, Medicine Creek, Jefferson, Johnson and Maloney.

In Ancient Ages

Several times in past ages the land now called Nebraska must have been at the murky bottom of inland seas. Each time after the land was covered with water, forces deep inside the earth raised the ground upward until the sea waters drained off. Sometimes in these periods between the seas the climate was almost tropical, and tropical plants and animals lived on the land. The most recent of these changes (about 60,000,000 years ago) was the Rocky Mountain uplift, which formed our greatest western range. Nebraska was on the eastern edge of this mighty lifting of the land, and the land that now forms the state was tilted downward to the east as its neighbors to the west rose even higher. None of the great mountains thrust through the surface of Nebraska, as they did in neighboring Colorado, Wyoming and even South Dakota. The newly formed slope of the land made the waters run more rapidly, forming many new streams.

During the ice ages, only two of the great continental glaciers reached what is now Nebraska and these covered only portions of eastern Nebraska.

"Stone Bones"

As the seas came and went, the plants, animals and fish that lived there died and sometimes left their skeletons. Some of these turned to stone over the years, becoming what famed Chief Red Cloud called "stone bones." Nebraska is one of the greatest "hunting grounds" for these stone bones or fossils.

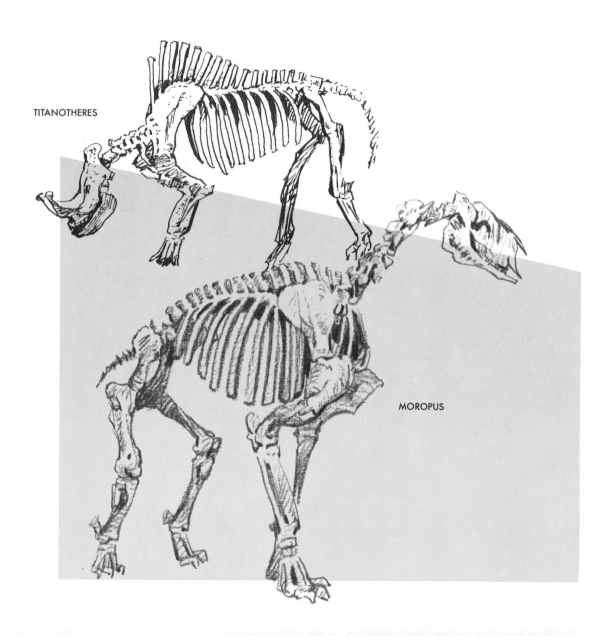

TITANOTHERES

MOROPUS

An expert named Leidy heard Red Cloud talking about these stone bones and began to study them. As early as 1850 he wrote a book about the region's fossils, *Ancient Fauna of Nebraska*. Captain James H. Cook made fossil discoveries at a later date, and he established his ranch near them. These are now the famous Agate Springs Fossil Quarries. Many of the discoveries were housed in the Cook Museum of Natural History nearby. Other famous Nebraska fossil quarries are Devil's Gulch and Hay Springs.

Probably nowhere has there been a wider variety of fossils found than in Nebraska. Many had been previously unknown and could not be identified with any living things. One of these was a huge shovel-tusked mastodon. Other fossils found in Nebraska include the rhinoceros-like great titanotheres, pig-like animals known as oreodonts, and another primitive tusked pig known as donohyus, six-feet high. The clumsy relative of the horse called moropus has been found and giant beavers, large turtles, camels, and crocodiles. Paleontologists are positive that more will be found as exploration continues.

Climate

Due to their height, the western tablelands of Nebraska are generally cooler than the eastern plains. However, throughout the state temperatures vary quickly in a manner common to most far-inland regions. The warm winds known as chinooks often blow across northwest Nebraska, which makes this area somewhat more moderate during the winter. The proportion of sunny days is high, and humidity is generally low.

Rainfall varies from about 30 inches per year in the southeast to around 16 inches in the west. Average rainfall for the state as a whole is 22.84. Since the rains come mostly in May, June and July, Zebulon Pike was led to write about the "barren soil, parched and dried up for eight months in the year." However, the rains come generally during the best period for crops.

Collecting Your Thoughts

Many different forces have helped to form the Nebraska of today; make a list of these forces with the changes each of these has made.

Footsteps on the Land

Prehistoric and Protohistoric Peoples

No spectacular ruins of ancient cities or other such evidences of ancient civilizations have been found in Nebraska. However, over the years a good many items have been found which tell about some of the peoples who made the area their home long ago.

The oldest group known to have been in the Nebraska region was called Folsom People. Their beautifully carved arrow and spearheads, known as Folsom points, have been found. Because Folsom relics have been found in connection with such extinct animals as an ancient bison skeleton, it is assumed that these people hunted the now extinct animals once found on the plains, such as the mammoth, musk ox and ancient bison.

Probably there were people in Nebraska before the Folsom culture; there have been many groups since. These include the Sterns Creek Culture, Upper Republican Culture and Nebraska Culture. Near Plattsmouth have been found relics of the Sterns Creek people. Their carved antelope horns show that they knew how to work in bone and make pottery. They apparently grew some crops and made their houses of poles, bark and reeds. Nebraska Culture people left enough bone hoes and other agricultural instruments to show that they were probably good farmers. They made brownish-red pottery of many sizes and uses.

Among the especially interesting prehistoric remains in Nebraska are the ancient flint quarries found near Nehawka. Prehistoric mounds called stone cists are found near O'Neill. These were burial boxes formed from limestone slabs, which have been set in shallow dugouts and covered with dirt. Inside the mounds have been found implements, jewelry of bones and shells, stone hatchets and spearheads.

Ionia "Volcano" near Ponca is not a volcano. It is a high bluff on the Missouri River; chemicals in the clay of the bluff react with water and form a smoke or steam. The prehistoric people who lived in the region considered the "volcano" sacred. Some accounts say that the old, the sick, prisoners of war or others were tortured and then sacrificed to the gods who controlled the volcano.

Eight Tribes

Eight major tribes of Indians were found by the first explorers in Nebraska. They were the Pawnee, Omaha, Oto, Ponca, Sioux, Cheyenne, Arapahoe and Missouri.

The Pawnee were present in the largest numbers. As late as 1800 there were estimated to be more than 10,000 Pawnee in what is now Nebraska. They were primarily farmers, raising beans, corn and melons as well as tobacco. After the women planted the crops in the spring, the whole tribe would go off on a major buffalo hunt, and the crops would have to care for themselves. They built circular lodges, sometimes as much as 60 feet in diameter. The floor of these lodges was generally below the level of the ground. In the center was a crude fireplace. The smoke escaped through a hole in the roof. The supports of logs were covered with mud to make firm walls.

The village formed the important unit of tribal organization. The village council was made up of chiefs, who inherited their title, and other leaders of the village. Medicine men were charged with the care of the sacred objects of the village and with the many ceremonials. Tribes were made up of several villages, with a tribal council of representatives from the village councils. The entire Pawnee nation was governed by a grand council made up of the members of the various tribal councils. The great united Pawnee nation included the following principal divisions: Kitkehaki (Republican Pawnee), Chaui (Grand Pawnee), Skidi (Loup or Wolf Pawnee), and Pitahauerat (Noisy Pawnee).

Buffalo hunts were organized by tribes, and there were officials who kept order and took charge of the distribution of the meat so that no family was left out. The meat was cut in narrow strips, dried by a process called jerking, and stored in containers called parfleches.

The Pawnee were noted for their elaborate ceremonials. Almost every daily activity was observed with some kind of ceremony.

All hair on the braves' heads was shaved off except for a narrow ridge of hair over the top of the head; this scalp lock was known as a pariki. Some form of the word pariki may have given the Pawnee their name. Hair of the women was tightly woven into two braids worn down

the back; they reddened the part of their hair as well as their cheeks.

Most of the other Indian tribes found by early explorers in Nebraska were smaller in number and had migrated to the area in comparatively recent times. The Omaha were among the most gentle and friendly. They had no war chiefs and seldom went on the warpath. However, one of their chiefs, Blackbird, was known for his cruelty to his own people. According to legend, he poisoned many who opposed him. Blackbird started the pirate custom, later followed by the Sioux, of stopping travelers on the Missouri and trying to collect a fee before letting them proceed. He died during a plague of smallpox which killed so many of the Indians of the region.

Working closely with the white people, the Omaha nation was served by many notable and worthy leaders. Big Elk was one of America's most far-seeing chiefs. He did a great deal to prepare his people for white rule, which he saw could not be avoided. He adopted a son of Ponca and French background, called Iron Eye (Joseph La Flesche), who succeeded him. He also ruled his tribe with wisdom. When the Winnebago were driven out of their traditional homes in the north and east, the Omaha kindly took in some groups of them and gave them lands for their use.

The Ponca were considered to be among the most successful of all Indian farmers of the region. The Missouri and Oto were related tribes of Sioux background. The principal Oto village near present Ashland had about 200 lodges of earthen construction. They also were a peaceful people, noted for their burial customs. Old women of the tribe dug the graves, only wide enough to hold the bodies in a sitting position, and the same old women conducted the funeral services. Afterwards the grave opening was covered with sticks and a buffalo robe, and then dirt was piled on top. Often a pony would be strangled and left on the grave for the coyotes and carrion birds. The bleached pony skull would be placed on the grave as a marker, along with the tail hairs tied to a stick. When graves could not be dug, the dead were placed in the limbs of trees. Some oak trees near the Oto villages were found to contain the mummies of many Indians wrapped in animal skins and tied tightly to the tree limbs.

Less settled, wilder and more brutal were the Indians of the western plains of Nebraska—Arapahoe, Cheyenne, and the fierce Sioux. These plains Indians considered that most of the state was their hunting ground, and so they terrified not only the white settlers but also the Indian tribes to the east. Warfare between the Pawnee and the Sioux almost never ceased. The Pawnee kept up running battles also with the Crow, Arapahoe, Cheyenne, Osage, Comanche, and Kiowa.

Casual Visits

Tales of a great city, with streets paved of gold, lured Spanish explorer Coronado into the American plains in 1540 and 1541, and he once was thought to be the first European to set foot on what is now Nebraska. This is now not thought likely. Spanish explorer-colonizer Don Juan de Onate may have visited present Nebraska in 1598.

When the English colonies of Virginia, Connecticut and Massachusetts were established on the eastern coast of America, they claimed that their territory extended as far west as the western seas. If the claim had been allowed, this would have put the future city of Omaha in Connecticut, among other strange tricks of geography.

Through the explorations of Robert Cavalier, the Sieur de La Salle, the French claimed vast regions of America which included Nebraska. The Spanish did not recognize these claims; although little is known about this, it appears that groups of both French and Spanish wandered through the region for many generations. The French helped their Pawnee Indian allies in the area, and the Spanish were aided by the Navajo and others. In 1699 a group of Navajo appeared in Spanish towns carrying French trophies and praising the French for their courage. The Spanish claimed to know that there were French settlements on a large river thought to be the South Platte.

In 1720 Pedro de Villasur took a good-sized force from Santa Fe to drive out the French. On August 14, the Pawnee attacked them, killed Villasur and large numbers of his men somewhere along the Platte, possibly near present North Platte or Columbus. In 1739, French brothers Paul and Pierre Mallet are said to have named a river the Platte, which is the name it still bears, and traveled along its banks for about 12 days, crossing most of what is now Nebraska before turning southwest and finally arriving at Santa Fe.

When the English won the French and Indian War, the French gave up all their claims, leaving the Spanish in sole possession of all the vast lands west of the Mississippi. At the end of the American Revolution, lands of the United States reached as far west as the Mississippi, making a common frontier with Spanish possessions across the river, with the whole region known as Louisiana. In 1801 Napoleon forced

23

Spain to return all of Louisiana to France, in the Treaty of Madrid. Three years later in one of the most important and ingenious real estate deals of history, the United States was able to buy Louisiana from France.

"The Most Beautiful Which I Ever Beheld"

President Jefferson sent Meriwether Lewis and William Clark to explore the new land. Their party of about 50 men pushed up the Missouri and as Clark wrote in his diary, "arrived at the mouth of the great Platte River at 10 o'clock (on July 21, 1804). This great river, being much more rapid than the Missouri, forces its current against the opposite shore. The current of this river comes with great velocity, rolling its sands in the Missouri, filling up its bed. . . . Captain Lewis and myself with six men in a pirogue went up this great river Platte and about two miles . . . passing through different channels, none of them more than five or six feet deep. . . .

"I am told by one of our Party who wintered two winters on this river, that 'it is much wider above, and does not rise more than five or

six feet,' spreds verry wide and . . . cannot be navigated with Boats or Perogues. The Indians pass this river in Skin Boats which is flat and will not turn over. The Otteaus (Oto) a small nation reside on the South Side 10 Leagues up, the Panies (Pawnee) on the Same Side 5 Leagues higher up."

Among the interesting visits made by the explorers was one to the grave of fierce malevolent Chief Blackbird, who had died four years before. On July 30, Captain Clark wrote that he had found "the most butifull prospect of the River up and Down the Countrey opposit presented it self which I ever beheld." They sent out many invitations to the Indians to meet with them, and on August 3, although most of the Indians were gone on their annual buffalo hunt, they held a council with some of the Missouri and Oto, at the Council Bluffs on the Nebraska side, "Delivered a long speech to them expressive of our journey, the wishes of our Government. Some advice to them and Directions how they were to conduct themselves. . . . Those Chiefs all Delivered a Speech . . . that they wer happy to find that they had fathers which might be depended on, ec."

On August 18 a party sent to capture some deserters returned to camp with M. B. Reed, one of the deserters, and three principal Oto chiefs. Reed was tried and "Sentenced him to run the Gantlet four times through the Party & that each man with 9 Swichies should punish him. . . . The three principal Chiefs petitioned for Pardin for this man after we explained the injurey such men could doe them by false representations and explaning the customs of our Countrey they were all Satisfied with the propriety of the Sentence & was Witness to the punishment."

On September 7, Lewis and Clark made their last camp in Nebraska and went on up the Missouri. Just two years later, after one of the most successful explorations of all time, they returned. Clark made a comment in his diary for September 5, 1806, about an Indian custom: "the report of the guns which was heard must have been the Mahars (Omaha) who most probably have just arrived at their village from hunting the buffalow. This is a season they usialy return to their village to secure their crops of corn Beens punkins &c."

Modest Beginnings

Almost on the heels of Lewis and Clark came trappers, traders and soldiers. In 1805 trader, explorer, and merchant Manuel Lisa made his first of many trips up the Missouri in search of furs and other trade. In 1807 Lisa found the site of Bellevue which later was to become the first permanent settlement in present Nebraska. Manuel Lisa is sometimes known as "the father of Old Nebraska."

When renowned Zebulon Pike went westward in 1806, he held a grand council on the Republican River. More than 400 Indians attended and Pike succeeded in making them lower the Spanish flag and raise the American. The exact location of this successful meeting has never been precisely determined. Kansas claims that it took place in present Kansas, and Nebraska is equally certain that it was in Nebraska. Regardless of the location, after Pike's journey Spanish authority was broken in the area.

In 1811 Wilson Price Hunt and his party went up the Missouri River on their way overland to establish Astoria in Oregon. The next year Robert Stuart led a party back from Astoria. On a very difficult journey they entered present Nebraska, after spending the winter in Wyoming. They could not float down the shallow Platte in canoes, so they loaded their goods on an old horse bought from the Snake Indians. When they reached an island of 70 miles in length, they recognized this landmark as Grand Island. At an Indian village nearby, they met some white traders, traded their horse for a canoe and floated down the Platte and the Missouri. Their travels brought valuable new knowledge about the Platte Valley.

On Manuel Lisa's annual trip up the Missouri in 1812, he established Fort Lisa, about ten miles north of present Omaha. The first treaty between the United States and the Pawnee was agreed upon in 1818. Fort Atkinson became the first settlement by Europeans in the present state, but it lasted only until 1827. At its beginning it was the most remote outpost of the United States. In 1823 Peter Sarpy established an American Fur Company post at Bellevue, south of present Omaha. This proved to be the first permanent European settlement in what is now Nebraska.

The first wagon passed across the Nebraska region in 1824 with the William Ashley party. In the Treaty of Fort Atkinson, September 25, 1825, the Pawnee acknowledged the federal government. However, the land of the region had not been opened for settlement, and the principal activity of those outside the Indian tribes was trading with those tribes for furs.

Missionaries were the next group in Nebraska. The Baptist Missionary Union established a mission in 1833 at Bellevue to convert the Oto Indians. Moses Merrill preached the first sermon in what is now Nebraska in that year. A Presbyterian mission was located there several years later.

Father Pierre Jean de Smet was the first Catholic missionary in the area, arriving in 1836. Visiting the Oto village near present Papillion, he was given a banquet by the First Chief. The "Queen" gave him a seat on a cushion "shining with grease." The meal consisted of a sort of stew and kind of pie; he did not want to offend them by refusing, so he said to himself, "Well, well, you are not in Belgium; let us begin our apprenticeship in earnest, and so long as we are in the woods, howl heartily with the wolves." The stew was made of buffalo tongue floating in a gravy of bear fat, thickened with wild sweet potato flour. Much to his surprise he found it "really excellent," and he described with amusement the number of dogs which sat around watching every mouthful with envy.

Father de Smet traveled throughout almost the entire West in his many years of extraordinarily fruitful service, crossing present Nebraska four times in all. He made 17 passages up the Missouri River, water border of Nebraska. The Pathfinder, John C. Frémont, crossed Nebraska. Frémont and his guide, Kit Carson, carved their names in a rock on the bank of Rock Creek near Fairbury, but this interesting historical reminder can no longer be seen there.

Wagons Westward!

In the period that followed, Nebraska was important mainly as a highway to the West as an incredible movement of pioneers began across the plains. The first major movement was the trek to Oregon, crossing Nebraska on part of what came to be known as the Oregon Trail.

Later, the Mormons were driven from their homes in Illinois, and in the winter of 1846-1847 more than 6,000 of them camped in a temporary town known as Winter Quarters, built on both the Iowa and Nebraska sides of the Missouri River near present Council Bluffs, Iowa, and Omaha. In the spring the first of these Mormon pioneers started across Nebraska, followed by more and more over a period of many years. The Oregon Trail and the Mormon Trail came together in Nebraska, although on opposite sides of the Platte River. The Oregon Trail followed very much the route blazed by the Stuart Astorian party more than 30 years before. The Mormon Trail followed much the same route as present Highway 30 across the state.

A journal writer on one of the wagon trains described the scene at one of the camps: ". . . a singular spectacle. The hunters returning with the spoil; some erecting scaffolds, and others drying the meat. Of the women, some were washing, some ironing, some baking. At two of the tents the fiddle was employed in uttering its unaccustomed voice among the solitudes of the Platte; at one tent I heard singing; at others the occupants were engaged in reading, some the Bible, others poring over novels. While all this was going on that nothing might be wanting to complete the harmony of the scene a Campbellite preacher, named Foster, was reading a hymn, preparatory to religious worship. The fiddles were silenced, and those who had been occupied with that amusement, betook themselves to cards. Such is but a miniature of the great world we had left behind us, when we crossed the line that separates civilized man from the wilderness. But even here the variety of occupation, the active exercise of body and mind, either in labor or pleasure, the commingling of evil and good, show that the likeness is a true one."

The emigrants used buffalo skulls for writing paper, leaving them along the side of the trail with the names of people of their party and any instructions that might be helpful to those who were coming later. Troublesome stream crossings were described; sites for pasturage and locations of wood were detailed.

In order to keep track of how far they had traveled William Clayton, of the first Mormon party to cross Nebraska, was assigned to the tedious task of counting each revolution of the wheel; at the end of the day the distance was computed on the basis of the circumference of the wheel multiplied by the number of revolutions. Before the journey was over, however, Appleton Harmon designed a sort of pioneer "roadometer," which proved a great success and relieved Clayton of his counting tedium.

The next great group of emigrants were those who came in 1849, straining every resource to reach California in time to make a strike in the gold fields. Crossing the Platte in 1849, "The line (of wagons) for two miles along the river bank presented as busy an aspect as it ordinarily does in St. Louis, or any other small town in the States," according to one emigrant's journal.

"Four boats, each consisting of two dug-outs fastened together, had been made by emigrants who had crossed before and gone on, others buying their rights and continuing the work. We paid $3 per wagon for the use of the boats, and swam the oxen. . . . Our 'boat' was called the *Two Pollies and Betsy,* from their being two dugouts, with a log between them. Joining forces with the twelve Cincinnati mule trains, the boat started off in style with 30 men to cordelle it against the current. The men were obliged to work in the water, which rendered it quite unpleasant; but by 4 o'clock we were across, and then drove the oxen down to swim.

"With all of our efforts, swimming and wading from that time until dark, we could only get three of them across; so had at last to let them return to the shore, and were obliged to keep watch of them until morning. . . . Again resumed our labors. . . . Fancy for one moment our feelings on observing the vast aggregation of oxen, mules, horses and wagons mixed indiscriminately with men, clothed, half-clad and even almost naked, encountering the elements that were temporarily stopping our progress. . . .

"The onlookers witnessed sights ranging from the laughable to the alarming. In one place six men were assisted ashore by hanging to the tail of a mule, with a rider on him. A boat with a wagon containing women and children sank but was saved by striking a bar. I was carried by the swift current outside the jam of cattle, and saved myself by catching hold of the tail of an ox as I passed him, and letting him tow me to shore."

Nebraska Territory

The last great group of pioneers in wagon trains came for many decades, sometimes in an almost unending stream of wagons. These were the early settlers of Nebraska.

In 1844 an effort was made to have a territory of Nebraska created, but this was defeated because those who favored slavery were alarmed over the prospect of a new free state. Ten years later, on May 30, 1854, Congress passed the Kansas-Nebraska Act proposed by Senator Stephen A. Douglas; this provided for what it was supposed would eventually be the slave state of Kansas and the free state of Nebraska.

President Franklin Pierce chose Francis Burt as first governor of the territory, but he died only two weeks after he arrived, and Thomas B. Cuming became acting governor. In 1855 the first legislature met at Omaha City, which had been founded just the year before. Omaha served as the capital until 1867. The first census showed that 2,732 people lived in the territory; however, it was vastly larger than the present state of Nebraska, including Kansas and portions of the Dakotas, Colorado, Wyoming, and Montana.

After the territory was established, more settlers came in. There were a few slaves in Nebraska, but many settlers were opposed to slavery. The underground railroad, secretly bringing slaves from the slave states up through the free states to safety in Canada, operated vigorously in Nebraska. John Brown, the most active foe of slavery, brought many groups of Negroes from Kansas through Nebraska and on to freedom.

When the Civil War came, the territory was not well enough developed to play a large part, but the First Regiment of Nebraska was enrolled on June 8, 1861, and altogether 3,307 from what is now Nebraska served in the Civil War, out of a total population of only 30,000. It is interesting to note that Omaha and Pawnee Indians served in the army as scouts.

During the war, in 1862, the first Homestead Act was passed. This provided up to 160 acres of land free to people who claimed that amount of land, lived on it for the required five-year period of time, and made certain improvements. Several claims have been made in various states as to who was the first person in the country to claim Homestead land; it is almost impossible to be certain who was really the first. However, Nebraska's claim is based on the application of Daniel Freeman, near Beatrice. The land office was not officially open until January 2, 1863, but Freeman was scheduled to leave for military service the night of January 1. By accident he met the young man who operated the land office and told him the story. He took Freeman to

32

the office and allowed him to make his claim just after midnight, so that if any others were earlier, it could hardly have been by more than a few seconds or minutes.

After the would-be homesteader had found a suitable claim, the first step was to travel to the land office, often more than 100 miles away; if he were slow in filing, someone else might beat him and file a claim to the land he wanted. The Beatrice *Express* gave a graphic description of the Beatrice land office: "The jam was terrible, and the poor woman was obliged to beg for more room from fear of fainting. The applications poured in as fast as they could be taken care of all day, the crowd inside and out never growing smaller, for as fast as one applicant, with papers properly fixed up, would worm his way through the crowd to the door, and be cast out, panting and dripping with perspiration, another would squeeze in, and became part of the solid, surging mass within."

Many of those taking land in Nebraska were veterans of the Civil War who were looking for new frontiers after their release from sevice.

Statehood

By 1864 the borders of Nebraska had been reduced almost to their present locations. In 1866 Congress passed a bill giving statehood to Nebraska. President Andrew Johnson vetoed the bill, but Congress passed the Nebraska statehood bill over the President's veto, and Nebraska became the nation's 37th state on March 1, 1867. David Butler was the first governor of the State.

The location of the state capital was the cause of many quarrels. Finally, the legislature appointed a special committee under Butler, and they chose a location in the middle of the wide open prairie near a small village known as Lancaster. This was to become Lincoln, the present capital of the state.

Collecting Your Thoughts

Choose several of the important exploring parties that passed through Nebraska that you would like to have joined. What do you think would have been the most important thing you would have learned from each of them?

Yesterday and Today

Indian Wars

As more and more covered wagons of settlers trundled across the prairie, the Indians watched stealthily and with growing alarm from such historic spots as Sioux Lookout southeast of North Platte. If the white man continued to come in, it became apparent that soon there would be no room left for the Indians on the hunting grounds that had so long been theirs.

From 1854 until 1877 across the plains, including Nebraska, there was almost constant war or trouble with the Indians. There were many immediate reasons for individual troubles, but the one great cause was simply the fact that sooner or later the Indians would be driven from their homes.

The period was a time of terror for settlers and travelers across the plains. Typical of the massacres was that of the five children of Henson Wiseman, killed near Wynot by a party of Sioux in 1863. Wiseman was serving in the army and learned of the tragedy a month after it happened. From that time on, he shot every Indian he saw and arranged their bodies as if in prayer.

The Frank Morton party from Iowa was attacked near present Lexington in August, 1864. Morton and eleven other men of the party were killed, and Morton's wife was held prisoner for five months. In another attack near Lexington, Chief Turkey Leg wrecked a freight train, scalped the crew and took the contents of the freight cars. The braves made a bizarre sight galloping across the prairie with bolts of colorful calico streaming from their saddles.

One of the strangest experiences of Indian attack was that of the Martin brothers. Indians attacked Martin and wounded him; his two sons jumped on their pony and dashed off with the Indians in pursuit. The story is told that one of the arrows hit one of the boys in the back, went through him and into his brother's shoulder, pinning the two boys together. One of them fainted and they fell from the pony. The Indians thought they were dead and left them there. However, the boys were soon found by their family, separated, and nursed back to health.

Periodically the army forces would bring the Indians under control

34

for a time. General George A. Custer skirmished with a large Indian group near Benkelman in 1867, nine years before he was killed at the Battle of the Little Big Horn.

Not all Indian battles were between the two races. In 1873 a group of about 300 Pawnee warriors and 400 women were hunting under the supervision of the government agent. Spotting a plain filled with buffalo, they hurried to the spot only to find that Sioux and Brule warriors had disguised themselves in buffalo robes. The Pawnee women hurried to a canyon where they chanted the victory and death song. However, the Pawnee men were overpowered and were only spared complete destruction by the coming of the cavalry. Bodies of 65 Pawnee were buried in one grave, and the tribe was never able to go on the hunt again.

In the 1870's the government began to move the tribes to Indian Territory in what is now Oklahoma. The Ponca refused to leave their homes, but were taken by force, herded like animals across the plains under the troopers' guns. There were no roads, and the captives left a trail of red from sore and bleeding feet. Many fell sick. At Milford a tornado ripped their tents to shreds and destroyed their wagons. There, too, Prairie Flower, daughter of Chief Standing Bear, died.

The Ponca found their new home mostly a land of hot and jagged rocks. Within a year 158 of Standing Bear's people died. Thirty of those who were left gathered their few possessions together and started back to their old homes. After ten weeks of fighting to survive, they came to the land of the Omaha and were taken in by them. However, they were ordered back to Indian Territory.

Two lawyers, John L. Webster and Andrew J. Poppleton, heard of their plight and took their plea to court. In one of the few cases of its kind, the Indians won, and the government was forced to permit them to stay in Nebraska. Their number has grown to about 300. The remainder of the tribe stayed on in Oklahoma.

None of the major battles which ended the Indian wars for all time was fought on Nebraska soil. However, one of the most dramatic events of the closing days of the war occurred at Fort Robinson. Thousands of the Indians, led by their chiefs, were streaming to the fort, to surrender and be placed on reservations. Many of them were following one of the great Indian chiefs of all time—the famed Crazy Horse. At the fort, it was said that at the last minute Crazy Horse refused to submit to capture and was run through and killed by the bayonet of one of the soldiers. The day of Indian mastery was over for all time.

The bid for freedom of the Cheyenne is another great epic of the frontier. They had been sent to Indian Territory in 1877, but they escaped and made their way through Kansas and into Nebraska before they were captured once more and brought to Fort Robinson. The rest of the story is told by J. Greg Smith in *Outdoor Nebraska:* "When told that his people must return to Oklahoma, Dull Knife (their Chief) replied, 'We are home. You may kill us, but you can never make us leave our land again.'

"Dull Knife's 149 men, women and children were imprisoned in log barracks at the southeast end of the post for three months. On January 9 (1877) they made their second heroic bid for freedom. Using their few concealed guns, they opened fire on the soldiers guarding the barracks, overpowered them, and took their arms and ammunition. While the women and children fled across the river, eight warriors fought off the alarmed garrison. Many Cheyenne fell between the barracks and the river but most escaped to the buttes where the battle continued for two weeks in Warbonnet, Smiley, Hat Creek, and Sowbelly canyons.

"The Cheyenne Outbreak Battle is one of the ironies of the frontier. Many of the Cheyenne had been fighting for, not against, the army only two years before. General Crook considered them 'among the bravest and most efficient' of those who fought under him and Mackenzie against the Sioux in 1876 and '77."

Only one white man, George Rawley, had been killed in the Cheyenne's march across Nebraska. After the battles, the Cheyenne returned to the Red Cloud Indian agency at Fort Robinson.

A Growing State

In spite of all the trouble with Indians during the period, the state continued to grow. The most important single reason for growth was the coming of the railroad. Beginning at Omaha, one by one the ties were laid, and one by one the gleaming metal rails were placed on them; slowly the tracks replaced the ruts of the old trails, as the thou-

sands of workers toiled under the watchful eye of troops protecting them from the Indians.

Fortunately for the early growth of Nebraska, the route of the great new railroad, first ever to span the width of a continent, was laid across the heart of the state, with the Union Pacific crossing Nebraska and hurrying on to meet the other line from the west in Utah. The part of the incredible task in Nebraska was finished in 1867.

One of the principal early jobs of the railroad was to receive cattle which had been driven up over the trails from Texas. Nebraska was not on the main Chisholm cattle trail, but an extension led into Nebraska, and Schuyler was one of the first points on the Union Pacific from which great numbers of cattle were shipped. Ogallala was another important early shipping point for Texas cattle. After the cowboys had delivered their herds to the railroad towns, they usually looked for entertainment and celebration. Some of the Nebraska cattle towns were as rip-roaring as Dodge City and other more famous names.

From 1870 to 1890 the railroads did all they could to encourage settlers in Nebraska, knowing that the more people living there the greater their business would be. As the number of farmers and small land claims increased, the cattle ranchers with their great unfenced spreads of land became more and more disturbed. Rivalry between cattlemen and farmers grew increasingly intense. Fence wires were cut; there were killings on both sides, and constant cattle rustling decreased the herds of ranchers. When cases of disputed ownership of land came to court, cattlemen were generally beaten by the homesteaders because there were usually more farmers on the juries than cattlemen.

Both farmers and cattlemen complained about the practices of the railroads. Because they controlled the only practical means of marketing farm and ranch products, the railroads were accused of taking advantage of their monopoly by excessive rates and other unfavorable practices.

The worst grasshopper plague in the history of the region struck in 1874. Many settlers gave up in despair and left the country. The Indians stoically ground the hoppers into mash and ate a kind of grasshopper porridge.

A number of colorful events lifted the monotony of life on the frontier. One of these was the visit in 1872 of Grand Duke Alexis of Russia, who stopped at North Platte on his way to a buffalo hunt. The duke was 22 years old and the brother of the Czar of Russia at that time. To see that he got the greatest possible thrill from hunting America's biggest game, both General Phil Sheridan and Buffalo Bill Cody accompanied him. They made a camp in the bend of Red Willow Creek, near the camp of Chief Spotted Tail of the Sioux. To entertain the royal visitor, the chief and his men staged a brilliant war dance, and the duke killed several buffalo.

Another distinguished visitor was the Earl of Dunraven of England, who left Fort McPherson in 1874 with Buffalo Bill and 100 warriors on another buffalo hunt.

During the rush for gold in the Black Hills in 1876-1877, Sidney was the principal railroad stopping point for the overland trek to the Hills. As many as 1,500 eager gold seekers passed through Sidney in a day.

Nebraskans suffered, as did the rest of the nation, from the awful winter of 1880-1881, worst in the country's history.

Those who think the Midwest is lacking in art and culture might find it hard to explain that the first art association ever founded in the United States was begun at Lincoln in 1888. The year 1890 brought the twin disasters of a drought and financial crash, and in 1891, 18,000 prairie schooners of defeated or disgusted settlers reversed the trend of pioneer days and trundled out of Nebraska.

Nebraska helped a rival prairie community celebrate in 1893 when the western state organized a 1,000 mile horse race from Chadron to the Chicago World's Columbian Exposition. The race was won in the record time of 13 days, 16 hours. Nebraska held its own fair in 1898— the Trans-Mississippi International Exposition in Omaha. Heading the distinguished visitors was President William McKinley, who was more fortunate at this fair than he was at Buffalo, when he was assassinated at the fair there just three years later.

In 1904, the open range in Nebraska went into history with the passing of the Kinkaid Law, permitting homesteading of as much as 640 acres. One of Omaha's greatest tragedies occurred when the Easter tornado of 1913 caused loss of life and great damage.

A far greater disaster was World War I in which 47,801 from Nebraska served and which took the lives of 1,000 from the state. The inspiring Nebraska capitol building was begun at Lincoln in 1922. A year later, as a remembrance of the past, 100-year-old Chief Ruling-His-Sun at last was persuaded to sit down in his old age and smoke the pipe of peace with his ancient enemies the Sioux on the 50th anniversary of the Battle of Massacre Canyon which almost destroyed the Pawnee nation. Other members of both tribes have made this an annual occasion for pow-wow and the smoking of peace pipes.

In 1930, the Lincoln National Bank was the scene of one of the worst bank robberies in history, when about $2,000,000 was stolen from the vaults. Nebraska made transportation history in 1934 in another race from the state to another Chicago world's fair. The Burlington *Zephyr* made the pioneer run from Omaha to the Century of Progress Exposition in record time and inaugurated the age of the diesel streamlined train.

This was a period of mounting difficulties for the people of Nebraska; the great depression beginning in 1929 had been growing steadily worse; one of the worst droughts was adding further to the despair of farmers. Banks and insurance companies were foreclosing mortgages and taking the property of hundreds of farmers. Soon angry farmers began to stop the sale of foreclosed property with threats and even violence. The situation began to ease when the drought let up and emergency measures (such as mortgage moratoriums) were taken to keep the farmers on their land.

During World War II, 120,000 men and women from Nebraska were enrolled in the armed services of the United States. Of these, 3,839 lost their lives. Historic old Fort Robinson was used as a war dog training center during the war.

In 1957, just 100 years after it was first incorporated, Omaha adopted a new city charter. Because this charter "set the pace for forward-looking cities," Omaha was given an All-America city award in that year.

Full-scale participation in the Atomic Age came to Nebraska in 1963 when the Hallam plant south of Lincoln went into service as the nation's first sodium graphite reactor for the production of commercial power and energy. It produces electricity by atomic power. Large quantities of radiation with possible industrial uses are available as a by-product.

The People and Their Government

The government of Nebraska is unique in the entire United States. Where other states have legislatures divided into two houses, generally a house and senate as in the national Congress, Nebraska's legislature is made up of only one house. This is known as the unicameral system.

40

The 43 members of the Nebraska legislature are elected on a ballot which does not list them according to their party.

This unique system was originated by then State Senator J. N. Norton. In 1914 Addison E. Sheldon submitted a 48-page report on the plan. The report was debated for about 20 years. Then Senator George W. Norris threw his great influence toward the unicameral system and proposed a plan to accomplish it. The state constitution was amended by popular vote in 1934 to provide for a unicameral legislature of not less than 30 nor more than 50 members. Those who advocated the plan claimed that it would be more economical, would eliminate passing of responsibility from one house to another, and that many roadblocks and delays of a two-house body would be done away with.

The ethnic backgrounds of Nebraska people today are extremely mixed and not very distinct. The first immigrants from Europe to come in large numbers were from Germany, and there are more citizens of German background than any other in the state. Probably the next largest number of descendants are of Czech background, followed by Swedish, Danish, Russian, English, Irish and Polish.

Of the original settlers of the region, the Indians, about 4,000 remain today—only 10 per cent of the Indian population estimated in earlier times. About 300 Ponca live ten miles west of Niobrara, east of the Ponca about 1,200 Sioux, about 100 Sauk and Fox in southeastern Nebraska, and on separate tracts in Thurston County 1,175 Winnebago and 1,200 Omaha. The latter two are the only groups living on reservations in the state. Of the largest and most powerful group once occupying the state—the Pawnee—none remain.

An interesting custom is maintained by the Ponca. Each August they bring gifts to the Omaha tribesmen in memory of the kindness and generosity of the ancient Omaha people who gave a home to the displaced Ponca ancestors. Most of the Indians of Nebraska have adopted modern ways, although an occasional old custom may still be seen among the Winnebago. The Winnebago keep up their annual ceremonial dances at Winnebago in August, when they also celebrate other old customs, hold councils, revive ancient songs and legends. They keep up their traditional handicrafts in the making of bracelets

41

and rings, buckskin dresses and moccasins, bows and arrows, head-dresses and rugs.

Most of Nebraska's Indian children attend modern schools, and most of the younger generation wear modern clothing. Traditional Indian dress is seldom worn in the Omaha reservation, although beaded moccasins, bright shawls and braided hair are not uncommon among the older women. Most of the Omaha are Christians. They attend church at the Pentecost of the Blackbird (Dutch Reform) in Macy, one of the oldest places of worship in Nebraska.

The dead are remembered by feasts, prayers, and holy songs. Perhaps the most interesting tribute to their historic past among the Omaha is the annual Powwow Council, held in August in an oak grove near Macy. More than a hundred tents are put in place around a permanent council lodge of bark. To the thump of drums, the tribe's symbolic dances are performed. Traditions, myths and songs are part of the ceremonies. Much of the color and action of old Indian life is revived for a few days, and then the Omaha settle back into their usual lives as citizens of the space age.

The people of Nebraska are less than a hundred years removed from their pioneer past, and many experiences of that period still influence life today. The firmness of character gained by surviving the awful loneliness, the grinding poverty, the ceaseless toil, peril of Indians, grasshoppers, rattlesnakes, drought, floods, twisters, prairie fires of the early homesteads must certainly have been passed on to many of today's descendants of the pioneers.

The pioneer woman, especially, endured much. Mrs. N. M. Ayers, who settled in Furnas County as a bride in 1873, remembered some of her feelings fifty years later as she wrote, "We traveled all day over the vast prairies without seeing a tree or a shrub, not even a sage bush. I never longed to see a tree as I did that day. Our second day's drive brought us to Turkey Creek at noon and there for the first time since leaving Lowell we beheld the beautiful native trees for which we had been longing."

Pioneer life was usually begun in a dugout, scooped from the side of a hill—cramped, dirty and crawling with insects. If the claim had some timber, the fortunate settlers could build a log cabin. For most, the

pioneer home had to be built of "Nebraska marble," the tough, fibrous sod of the prairie. Blocks of sod a foot wide and up to a yard long were used. These were held together by the network of grass roots. The sod blocks were "laid" in much the same manner as bricks to form the walls, with dirt packed tightly between the blocks as mortar. Roofs were thatch or sod, supported on poles.

Those lucky enough to have them used boards for the floor; others had to be content with the bare ground. In times of plentiful rain, the exterior of a sod house presented a colorful sight of waving grasses, blooming weeds and riotous morning glories, with even a prairie rose or two blushing on the wall.

Prairie fires were only one danger of pioneer life. Mrs. M. A. Freas recalled how a fire once swept down on her sod house in Furnas County: "We all ran for our lives and arrived safely on the plowed ground (about 80 rods from the house). The flames rolled on around us and left us safe. I said, 'Let us pray God in His mercy and goodness to save our little home.' We did pray. Some said God had nothing to do with it, but I will always believe He did for our home was saved, although the ground was burned black around it."

In April of 1893, the entire 3,000 population of North Platte was threatened by an enormous prairie fire started by sparks from a railroad locomotive. With every able-bodied person fighting the fire, it was turned away after burning only about 35 houses.

The pesky grasshopper provided another pioneer plague. The Osceola *Homesteader* wrote in 1874, "Our foreign readers must forgive us for giving so much grasshopper news. We really cannot help it. The air is filled with them, the ground is covered with them, and people think and talk of nothing else. It rains grasshoppers and snows grasshoppers. We cannot walk the streets without being struck in the face and eyes by grasshoppers, and we cannot sleep for dreaming grasshoppers, and if the little devils do not leave for some other clime soon, we shall go grasshopper crazy."

The menace of the Indians was real and constant, but not all Indian invasions had tragic results. A favorite story on the frontier is retold by Fred Nelson in *Nebraskaland*. It concerned the "prairie wife who was surprised by 10 or 12 braves, probably Pawnee, as she was frying meat. The woman continued to cook as the Indians milled around the cabin, examining everything that caught their eyes. Some started to pilfer the cooked meat and the wife retaliated with a broom. She flew at the startled warriors like a skirted fury. The Indians practically took the door with them in their retreat from the broom wielding demon. They did not return."

Not all the settlers could take the hard times, and some returned to their former homes. A traveler near Columbus went to a prairie house for a drink of water. He found a sign which read: "This claim for sale. Four miles to the nearest neighbor. Seven miles to the nearest schoolhouse. Fourteen miles to the nearest town. Two hundred feet to the nearest water. God bless our home! For further information address Thomas Ward, Oskaloosa, Iowa."

However, most of the pioneers developed a fierce loyalty to their Nebraskaland. Many of them won over their land and began to enjoy a few comforts. When the first piano arrived at the Peter Sarpy home in Bellevue, the Indians often gathered in numbers outside the windows to watch and listen in wonderment.

Gradually most of the homesteads were improved and luxuries began to appear as the pioneers began to enjoy their hard-won gains, which were passed on in even greater measure to succeeding generations.

Collecting Your Thoughts

Many great changes have occurred in Nebraska since pioneer times.
Make as long a list of these as you can.

Natural Treasures

When Major Stephen H. Long passed Nebraska on his famous expedition of 1819, one of the members of his party wrote of the lands west of the Missouri as the "abode of perpetual desolation." This comment placed the great American desert on the map, and gave much of the West a reputation for barrenness which it came far from deserving.

Trying to correct this impression about Nebraska the Union Pacific Railroad printed brochures which spoke of the ". . . magnificent earth ocean . . . rolling up in beautiful billows along the shores of continental streams and mountains that border them . . . what used to be the Great American Desert . . . is actually the great national pasture ground . . . the Platte will prove to be the northern Nile. . . ."

However, even today large numbers of non-Nebraskans have an incorrect impression of Nebraska; as the state Game Commission points out, "Many outsiders regard Nebraska as a flat fertile plain that raises grain, cattle, an occasional dust storm and little else."

What none of the old observers could guess from a casual look was that Nebraska had wonderfully fertile soil (probably its greatest single asset) and that what appeared to be dry earth was really almost "floating" on a sea of water. This "sea" consists of the largest supply of underground water in the nation—an estimated 547 trillion gallons. If all of it could be brought to the surface, it would cover the whole state to a depth of 34 feet. In the days when supplies of fresh water are rapidly dwindling, this vast storage "tank" will certainly prove to be one of Nebraska's greatest sources of wealth—providing sparkling drinking water for an increasing population, irrigation for crops and water to supply the always thirsty manufacturing plants.

Among other minerals, sand and gravel are available in almost limitless quantities and there are many fine clays for bricks, ceramics and other commercial uses. The Hastings clay is especially useful for brickmaking. Proven supplies of oil and natural gas have increased as explorations have shown where these invaluable resources are to be found in the state.

In the early days, Nebraska was almost entirely a land without forest cover; today there are 250,000 acres of forest within the state. The story of how this came about is one of the fascinating tales of how man

GIANT COTTONWOOD NEAR GUIDE ROCK

has been able to aid Nature in the building of natural resources.

The native trees of the Nebraska area were mostly cottonwoods and willows. Cottonwoods grew to great size there, such as the "King of the Cottonwoods" in Guide Rock. Planted in 1871 by Mrs. Rhoda Simpson, the King is now almost 27 feet in circumference. Most of Nebraska's native trees were found along the streams, and most eastern trees found naturally in Nebraska migrated slowly up the Missouri River and other streams until they made their way into the Nebraska region. One of the finest stands of hardwood timber west of the Missouri River is found at Ponca State Park.

Tree-loving Nebraskans everywhere planted as many trees as they could. In 1860 William Stoley planted 6,000 trees, and this small forest is now the basis of Stoley State Park. Nebraska's eminent botanist Dr. Charles Bessey had a dream that forests would grow in Nebraska, even though Nature had not provided them. In 1902 he persuaded nature-loving President Theodore Roosevelt to establish the Nebraska National Forest. Of course, such a forest did not exist, but the plan was to demonstrate that forests could be planted on the Great Plains and to test the best kinds of trees for growth in such an area. Today the Nebraska National Forest boasts 22,000 acres of forest—the only forest in the world of any size entirely planted by man.

After the drought of the mid-1930's, the planting of shelter belts across the plains was another example of man aiding Nature instead of destroying natural wonders as he so often does. This kind of shelter belt not only checks wind erosion but furnishes timber.

The tall prairie grasses flourish in the eastern region; the short nourishing grasses grow in the western portion of Nebraska. The flowers and plants that grow in these two grass regions are very different. In the drier low grass region, cactus and other semi-arid regional plants are found. However, even the western tablelands are a riot of blossom in springtime when there have been good rains. Even in the Badlands and Brule Clay regions there are flowers, such as yellow umbels. In various parts of the state, wildflowers are abundant; one of the more spectacular is Frémont's primrose, with blossoms almost two inches in diameter. Wild rose, phlox, violet, spiderwort, yellow ladyslipper, columbine, waterlily, petunia, anemone, goldenrod and sunflower are found, along with many others.

The abundant grasses and groves of trees nourished by the waterways provide food and shelter for a surprising collection of animals and birds in the state.

Most spectacular, of course, were the buffalo, which have long since vanished except for a few herds raised by individuals or the state. So many millions of these huge snorting beasts once roamed the prairies that it is impossible for present-day people to appreciate the numbers. A Mormon writer, Appleton Harmon, gave a vivid description of buffalo in Nebraska. This provides an idea of their numbers:

"Had to drive the buffalo out of the way; whare we halted the buffalo seemed to form a complete line from the river their watering place to the bluffs as far as I could se which was at least 4 mi. (;) they stood their ground appurently amased at us until within 30 rods of the wagons when their line was broken down by some taking fright & running off (;) others to satisfay thar curiosity came closer within gun shot of the camp snuffing and shaking their shaggy heads, but being pursued by the dogs ranoff, at this time I could stand on my waggon & see more than 10,000 from the fact that the Plain was purfectly black with them on both sides of the river & on the bluff on our right which slopes off gradualy."

In 1837 artist Alfred Jacob Miller took careful note of the dimensions of a buffalo and wrote: "Length, seven feet, six inches; depth of body from top of hump to dewlap, four feet, five inches; length of head, three feet, two inches; height from hind foot to junction of tail, four feet, seven inches."

Most of the buffalo were exterminated by hunters over a short period of years. The meat was used by railroad workers and also helped many pioneers to exist; the skins were in great demand for robes; of course, there was great waste. However, it would not have been possible for the buffalo to continue to survive even if they had not been hunted. The coming of plowing and fences and other advances of "civilization" would have destroyed their home and their source of food, and they must certainly have died out or have been killed to protect new farms and ranches.

Some authorities feel that at one time elk may have been even more abundant than buffalo in Nebraska; however, there are no records on this. Mule deer and white-tail deer and pronghorn antelope were other once numerous native animals of the plains. Today only the smaller animals are found in any numbers.

More than 400 species of birds have been known in Nebraska. These range from the slender sandhills crane to the plump wild turkey. The native wild turkeys were killed off, but 28 were brought to Nebraska from other states in 1959, and now they are estimated to number 4,500. Other popular game birds are quail, prairie chicken and the hooded merganser duck "with its black and white suit." Another striking large black and white bird, sometimes surprisingly found in Nebraska, is the magpie.

However, an immigrant to Nebraska is probably the most numerous and popular of all the state's birds. In 1915 a few pheasants were imported from China. Nebraska's pheasant population today is estimated at an incredible five to six million.

Collecting Your Thoughts

Do you agree that good soil and abundant water are Nebraska's greatest natural resources? Give reasons for your answer.

People Use Their Treasures

"Beef State"—Agricultural Eminence

Marching head to tail in one long plodding line, the number of livestock traded in one year at Union Stockyards Company, Limited, at Omaha, would stretch twice across the entire United States. Omaha has replaced Chicago as the world's largest livestock market. In 1964 the number of animals traded at Omaha reached 6,305,231.

Nebraska ranks third among all states in total annual production of livestock and poultry. Livestock revenue in 1964 was $832,621,000. In that same year the state produced 6,004,000 head of what Nebraskans like to call "the best beef in the world." There were 2,640,000 hogs and 605,000 sheep. As early as 1817 English naturalist John Bradbury thought the plains, which were then considered useless, might someday have some value. He would be pleased to know how true his prediction was.

That same land in 1964 produced crops worth $400,536,100—ranking third in rye and sorghum grain, fourth in winter wheat, and fifth in corn. Total agricultural income of the state was $1,233,157,100. Three million acres of Nebraska farmland are irrigated.

Manufacturing, Mining and Minerals

The value of agricultural products still ranks considerably above that of manufacturing in Nebraska, but industry has shown a rapid rise in the state. Total value of manufacturing in Nebraska in 1963 was $757,000,000.

Much of the state's manufacturing is based on agriculture. The eighteen meat-packing plants in Omaha make it the largest meat-packing and processing center in the United States, taking over the title from its one-time rival, Chicago.

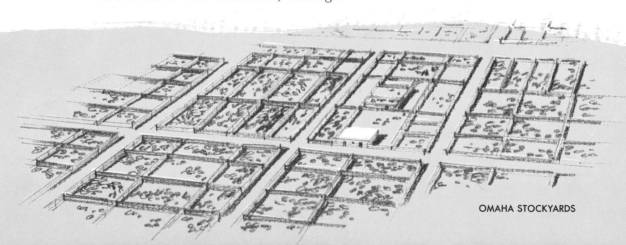

OMAHA STOCKYARDS

Omaha usually is considered the second largest food processing center in the world. The state's processed foods include canned fruits and vegetables, flour, soft drinks, malt liquors, candy, butter, cheese and ice cream, feeds for livestock and poultry, sugar, coffee, animal and vegetable fats and oils, spaghetti, noodles, macaroni, cereals, vinegar, gelatin, powdered milk, potato chips, and salad dressings. Omaha is one of the largest centers for processing frozen foods, especially the so-called "TV dinners."

Dawson County claims the title of "The nation's number one hay processor." Much of this is processed alfalfa. Like almost everything else, the alfalfa industry has been revolutionized. Instead of haystacks, "dehy" (dehydrating) plants line the roadsides. Trucks roll in with the green alfalfa directly from the fields. Six to eight ton loads of fresh-cut hay are digested in one gulp of a great chopper. Through grinders, bins, jets of air, furnaces at 2,000 degrees, and mills of several kinds the hay flows endlessly, and when it comes out after a thirty-minute trip through a raging furnace it is in the form of millions of green pellets of nutritious alfalfa hay—"green gold" as it has been called. Bagged or in bulk alfalfa pellets wind up as high year-round protein feed for the nation's livestock.

Nebraska turns out 567,100 tons of dehydrated alfalfa yearly, almost half of the total United States' production. The bulk of Nebraska's annual production of some four million tons of alfalfa finds its way into the state's 82 dehydrating plants. Each plant can have as high as a half dozen drums. Of the 350 or so drums in the United States, about 160 are in Nebraska. Of these, 63 are in Dawson County alone. At night the glowing cylinders of the furnace drums and the luminous smoke are bright beacons along the highway.

Other manufactured products include automobile parts and accessories, bedding, medicines, electrical machinery, communication equipment, air-conditioners, furniture, store fixtures, window shades and blinds, footwear, leather goods, millwork, tools, hardware, culverts, pipe, fencing, frozen-food lockers, grain bins, truck trailers, oil burners, farm equipment, wire, paper bags, roof materials, brick, tile, mirrors, monuments, glass cloth, cigars, boats, scooters, trailers, brooms, brushes, jewelry, toys, athletic goods, baker supplies, and refined metals.

Omaha has been a leading center of lead smelting. Nebraska is 15th among the 33 petroleum producing states. Natural gas is also important. However, production of both oil and natural gas is declining. Limestone is quarried in southeastern Nebraska for use as cut stone in buildings, in cement and as fertilizer. Sand and gravel, pumice, clay, and gem stones are produced. Mineral production in Nebraska totalled $93,900,000 in 1964.

Transportation and Communication

In 1865 General W. T. Sherman, fresh from his triumphs in Georgia in the Civil War, was on hand in Nebraska to help the then territory celebrate its first miles of railroad. The General and 20 other distinguished guests rode on a flat car along the beginning rail line from Omaha to Salings' Grove. They sat on nail kegs as the only available seats.

Nebraska land had first been broken for railroads in 1863, and the first rails laid two years later. During 1866, 250 miles of railroad were laid and in 1867 the final 240 miles were finished across the state. By 1869, Nebraska was on the main line of rail travel across the country. The first permanent railroad bridge was built over the Missouri River between Omaha and Council Bluffs in 1872.

There was much peril for early rail travelers across the prairies. Flimsy bridges might collapse at any time under the weight of a train; whenever a locomotive gained any considerable speed it was in grave danger of jumping the tracks; sparks frequently set the wooden cars on fire, and bandits on many occasions held up trains, robbed passengers and stole valuable cargo.

Today, Omaha is the fourth largest rail center in the United States and is still the general headquarters for the Union Pacific Railroad, the transcontinental rail pioneer.

As the great canoe that looked like a dragon puffing smoke moved slowly up the river, the Indians of Nebraska looked on in amazement that day in 1819. This was the first steamboat to travel on the Missouri, the *Western Engineer*. Under command of Major Stephen H. Long, it reached as far north as Fort Lisa above present Omaha. The designers had made the smokestacks of the boat in the shape of a dragon or serpent so that the Indians would be impressed and awed. The Indians thought they knew what had happened, explaining, "Whiteman, bad man, keep Great Spirit chained, built fire under him to make him paddle their boat."

By 1830 the American Fur Company had launched a fleet of shallow draft steamboats to travel the Missouri. There were the *Yellowstone, Omega, Assiniboin,* and *Nimrod.* By 1857, 50 steamboats ran on the Missouri as far north as Omaha. At the height of the Missouri steamboat period, in 1859, 268 boats were touching at Omaha. Brownville also starred as a river port.

As the river became more treacherous and more shallow and as the railroads took away the business, it seemed that Missouri River transportation was a thing of the past. Today a six-foot channel dredged in the Missouri makes Omaha a port once again. Barges propelled by busy towboats are bringing an increasing amount of freight up the river. Seven million bushels of grain, for example, were shipped from Omaha by barge in 1965. When the nine-foot channel is completed up the river, it is expected that Omaha will become an even more important inland port.

For "fast" and "dependable" transportation in the early days, the stagecoach was the thing. Famed stage line owner Ben Holladay was operating a daily stage across Nebraska over the Oregon Trail as early as 1861. Holladay broke the record for overland travel by stage, thundering between Salt Lake City and Atchison, Kansas, at the average speed of 160 miles per day with a cost running $10 per mile. In 1866 Wells Fargo bought out the Holladay company. Stagecoaches were still carrying passengers and freight in the Nebraska back country as late as 1900.

An interesting experiment in overland transportation was the great "steam wagon" made for Major J. R. Brown. With 10-foot drive wheels churning the dirt and smokestack belching clouds of smoke, the steam wagon made an impressive start as it lumbered out of Nebraska City in 1862, hauling 10 wagons over the prairie carrying 35 tons of freight. It lasted for 8 miles, broke down and never moved again under its own steam.

Today Nebraska boasts a network of interstate and other highways, many of them converging at Omaha. Right-of-way of the Platte Valley Parkway, a leading modern interstate express highway, is dotted with ponds and lakes. This man-made chain of lakes is designed to be a unique major recreation feature.

Omaha today is entered by 35 major truck lines, 9 major railroads and 5 major air lines. By air the city is 2½ hours from New York and 3 hours from Los Angeles.

The soil of Nebraska felt the hoof beats of one of the most famous means of communication in history—the glamorous Pony Express, which successfully carried the mail in the fastest time ever. The end of the Pony Express came with the arrival of another miracle of "modern" science—the telegraph. The August, 1860, issue of the New York *Times* noted that telegraph lines had reached "westward to the half-peopled wilds of Nebraska." When the line reached Brownville, the territory sent its greetings to the other states. Nebraska's first telephone line was installed between Omaha and Council Bluffs, Iowa, in 1877.

The state's earliest newspaper was the Nebraska *Palladium and Platte Valley Advocate,* established at Bellevue in 1854. A novel early newspaper was the *Pioneer on Wheels.* It took its name because it was printed in a boxcar at North Platte. Most prominent newspaper of the state is the Omaha *World-Herald.* This distinguished journal gained particular notice when William Jennings Bryan became its editor in 1894.

Collecting Your Thoughts

Choose one of the activities of Nebraska discussed above, find out more about it and list as many reasons as you can why it is important to the state.

Human Treasures

The Great Commoner

William Jennings Bryan was not a native of Nebraska, but for the largest part of his spectacular political career he was associated with the state, after moving to Lincoln in 1887, where he began a law practice. Bryan was elected to Congress from Nebraska in 1890, the first Democratic congressman from the state.

He soon became widely recognized for his gifts as an eloquent speaker, and was later considered one of America's greatest orators.

HOME OF
WILLIAM JENNINGS BRYAN

He joined the Chautauqua lecture circuit, and in a few years almost every community in the country had heard him speak. He promoted what was known as the free coinage of silver, and his most famous speech opposed the gold standard and was called the "Cross of Gold" speech. By the time of the Democratic national convention in 1896, he had become so prominent that he was the party's nominee for the Presidency, but was defeated by McKinley. However, Bryan remained the key leader of the Democratic Party until 1912.

In 1900 he again ran for President and was defeated by Theodore Roosevelt. In 1901 he founded the weekly paper *The Commoner,* to carry on his fight against the wealthy and powerful people he felt controlled American politics. After a round-the-world tour in 1905 and 1906, which gave him world renown, he ran for President in 1908 and was again defeated, this time by William Howard Taft.

He did not run for the presidency in 1912, but he was influential in getting the nomination of Woodrow Wilson. Bryan became Wilson's Secretary of State and served in that post until 1915.

Bryan's last appearance in the world spotlight was a strange one. A Tennessee teacher, John T. Scopes, had been arrested for teaching about evolution. Famed attorney Clarence Darrow defended Scopes. William Jennings Bryan was the principal attorney for the prosecution. This Scopes trial, one of the most famous in history, was won by Bryan, but he died a few days after its close and was buried at Arlington National Cemetery.

William Jennings Bryan's remarkable speeches fill thirty volumes.

George William Norris

Another famed political figure was a Nebraskan by adoption, George William Norris. He moved to Beaver City, Nebraska, in 1885 and became prosecuting attorney of Furnas County. He served his first term as a Republican Congressman from Nebraska and was elected to the Senate in 1913. Nebraska returned him to office for five straight terms. He served the state for a total of 47 years in Congress. Although he was elected as a Republican, for much of his period in office he considered himself an independent. Unafraid of party powers, he believed he owed explanations to no one but the voters who elected him.

A friend, J. E. Lawrence, wrote of him, "Virtually alone in the early 20's in one of the most conservative eras of American history, he carried on the discouraging battle which led to the ultimate establishment of the Tennessee Valley Authority. That victory established a sound, inspiring pattern for the conservation of natural resources, which has withstood a hundred powerful attacks. Twelve years of congressional battle went into it." One of the great dams of the Tennessee Valley, Norris Dam near Knoxville, was named in his honor.

Norris was against United States entry in World War I, but he supported the country's part in World War II. Among his important legislation were the Norris-La Guardia Anti-injunction Act and the Lame Duck amendment to the Federal Constitution in 1933.

In Nebraska, Senator Norris has been called the "greatest influence" in the creation of the unicameral legislature. He also was responsible for a series of dams for power and conservation in the Platte Valley. This has come to be known as the "Little TVA."

The book *Profiles in Courage,* written by President John Kennedy, includes Senator Norris as one of those Americans who stood by his beliefs in spite of great danger to his career. At the age of 81, George W. Norris was defeated for re-election, the first defeat in 47 years in public office. He returned to his home at McCook and spent his final years writing his autobiography, *The Fighting Liberal.* He finished this just eight weeks before his death in 1944.

Other Public Figures

In addition to his work for Arbor Day, Julius Sterling Morton made many other contributions to his nation and to his adopted state. In 1858 he became secretary of the Nebraska Territory and then acting governor. In 1893 President Grover Cleveland, at the start of his second term, appointed Morton as Secretary of Agriculture. He became the first person from Nebraska to serve on a President's cabinet.

Morton's oldest son, Joy, was the founder of the Morton Salt Company. Following in his father's footsteps he showed his interest in trees by donating the famed Morton Arboretum in Illinois, near Chicago, one of the finest and most complete collections of trees and shrubs in the world.

The second son, Paul, became Secretary of the Navy under President Theodore Roosevelt; he was also president of the Equitable Life Assurance Company.

In 1923, the Morton sons gave Arbor Lodge, the Morton estate at Nebraska City to the state, and it is now Arbor Lodge State Historical Park. This includes the Morton home, 52-room Arbor Lodge.

David Butler has been called the "foremost figure in early state politics." In 1871 he was impeached and removed from the office of governor, charged with illegally using state school money. He later paid back all the funds he was accused of taking, and in 1882 the people of his district showed their confidence in him by electing him as a state senator.

One of the most enduring of the state's political leaders was Tom Dennison, labeled Omaha's "boss" from about the beginning of the century until his death in 1934. It was said that he began his career as a gambler and got into politics to protect his gambling interests.

A prominent modern-day figure is Walter Judd, native of Rising City. Dr. Judd served as a medical missionary in China, becoming a leading authority on the Far East. He was elected to the House of Representatives from Minnesota for 10 consecutive terms.

Charles G. Dawes, Vice President of the United States and sponsor of the Dawes Plan, had law offices in Lincoln in the same building as William Jennings Bryan. During the same period in which Bryan and Dawes lived in Lincoln, one of America's best-known military men, General John J. Pershing, served on the staff of the University of Nebraska, instructing in military science.

Perhaps the largest fortune gained in Nebraska was that of George A. Joslyn of Omaha, whose wealth came from the operation of a newspaper cooperative service—The Western Newspaper Union. The Joslyn family gave the Joslyn Museum at Omaha to the city in memory of the family founder.

In the field of scholarship, law authority Dean Roscoe Pound has been called the "most learned man produced in the state." Another outstanding scientist and educator is George W. Beadle, President of the University of Chicago, born near Wahoo.

Creative Nebraskans

A number of America's best-known writers have been associated with Nebraska.

The parents of Willa Cather brought her to Red Cloud at the age of nine. Her writings not only gave her fame but have added wide understanding of the prairie region where she continued to make her home. Her book *O Pioneers,* published in 1913, marked the beginning of a long period of interest in literature about Nebraska. This book has been called "a memorable example of the modern regional novel." In 1923 Willa Cather was awarded the Pulitzer Prize for her novel *One of Ours.* One of her best-known works was *Death Comes for the Archbishop,* published in 1927.

Mari Sandoz grew up in Nebraska's Sandhills country. Her father, Jules Sandoz, came from Switzerland to be a Sandhills pioneer. Mari Sandoz' best-known book is *Old Jules,* based on the life of her father. For this she won the Atlantic Monthly Prize.

Novelist Bess Streeter Aldrich was another who liked to write about pioneer life on the prairies. In her book *A Lantern in Her Hand,* one of the true stories retold is that of Hangman's Tree near Murray. One of the best-known and most skillful mystery story writers is Mignon Good Eberhart, also from Nebraska.

Nebraska poet John Gneisenau Neihardt spent 30 years in preparation for and writing of his *The Cycle of the West.* This is a long five-"song" volume of epic poetry. Well-known names of the old west charge through the work "with real life and color." Neihardt graduated from Nebraska Normal College (Wayne State) at the age of 16. He spent much time with Omaha Indian tribesmen and added to his store of western lore. In 1921 he was named Poet Laureate of Nebraska by the legislature. This was the first time any state had ever made such an appointment. He is now widely known as "Poet of the West."

Edwin Ford Piper is another of Nebraska's better-known poets. His *Barbed Wire and Other Poems* told of the disappearance of the free cattle range.

Dr. Richard Tanner of Norfolk was an early plainsman who came to be known as "Diamond Dick." His adventures were fictionalized in the popular *Diamond Dick* novels that delighted so many young people of an earlier day.

It has been said that art in Nebraska has advanced from murals drawn by Indians on tepee walls to the most modern works of highly-trained artists in only about a hundred years.

Yosette La Flesche Tibbles, a part-Indian artist of the prominent La Flesche family, was born at Bellevue in 1854. She created many paintings and illustrated a book printed in 1898—*Oo-Mah-Ha Ta-Wa-Tha.* The drawings for this book are considered to be the first work by an Indian artist ever published. Charles S. Simmons of Scottsbluff gained a reputation as a painter of frontier scenes.

One of America's most distinguished composers and conductors, Howard Hanson, was a native of Nebraska.

Such Interesting People

In 1917 an Omaha priest borrowed $90 from a friend and began a career which made him into "an international symbol of spiritual and material hope for millions." The priest was the Right Reverend Monsignor Edward J. Flanagan, who became known all over the world as Father Flanagan.

Father Flanagan used the $90 for the first month's rent on an old house in Omaha. To this house he brought a growing number of homeless boys. The first Christmas after the home was opened, the Christmas dinner consisted mostly of a barrel of sauerkraut donated by a friend. Father Flanagan kept up the work, supported by gifts until the home was too crowded to continue and was moved to the old German Civic Center.

Operating almost entirely on hope, Father Flanagan acquired land near Omaha and moved his boys into temporary wooden barracks. Today Boys Town with a staff of 125 trained and experienced workers has fine high schools and grade schools, substantial dormitories for grade school boys, 25 cottage houses for high school boys and provides every facility for training boys and rehabilitating those who need it. The "alumni" of Boys Town now number more than 10,000.

Father Flanagan spent much time in later years advising and counseling organizations all around the world in how to deal with homeless or delinquent young people. He died in Germany in 1948, and Father Nicholas H. Wegner took over the direction of Boys Town.

William F. (Buffalo Bill) Cody has been associated with many states. He was already famous when he came to North Platte in 1870 to make his home. He was the most famed citizen of North Platte for almost thirty years. Scouts' Rest was the name of his ranch northwest of the town. Here he organized his world-traveling Wild West Show in 1883 and trained it there for the triumphs of its performances for kings and queens and everyday people everywhere.

In the tradition of Buffalo Bill, Nebraskan Jim Houston became the world's champion bronc rider in 1965.

The unselfishness of Samuel Allis deserves to be remembered. He had been robbed by the Indians at a time when he was "in distress and in a state of starvation." Later when the Indians were suffering terribly from smallpox, Samuel Allis forgot his former mistreatment and vaccinated more than 2,000 of the Pawnee tribe. The story has an even more unusual ending. When the Pawnee received $40,000 a year for five years to pay for a tract of land, the Indians insisted that Samuel Allis be given $1,000 because they "felt that he should be paid for these things."

An Omaha man who "gained several fortunes" and even greater fame as an eccentric was George F. Train. As an independent he ran for President of the United States in 1872. Publishing a newspaper in New York, Train was jailed for printing certain passages from the Bible which the courts said were obscene.

An unusual number of well-known entertainers have been Nebraskans. These include Harold Lloyd, Fred Astaire, Henry Fonda, Marlon Brando and Robert Taylor.

The modest fame of Fred Patzel of Norfolk is still remembered by some Nebraskans. In 1926 Fred won the national hog-calling contest. Demonstrating the skill that won his title over the local Norfolk radio station, his prize-winning bellow put the station completely off the air.

Collecting Your Thoughts

Select one of the personalities mentioned here to read about. Make as long a list as possible of facts which you have discovered.

Teaching and Learning

Nebraska has four universities, nineteen four-year colleges and seven colleges which offer less than a four-year program.

The largest institution for higher education in the state is the University of Nebraska in Lincoln. The Nebraska legislature provided for a state university in an act of February 16, 1869. The first building was completed at Lincoln in 1871. The staff included a faculty of four plus the chancellor. There were twenty students.

Today the university enrolls almost 10,000 and has branches in many parts of the state. On the most advanced level of education, the university operates the Nebraska Center for Continuing Education, housed in a striking structure designed to accommodate educational seminars and conferences. Each year hundreds of such meetings of distinguished scientists, educators and other authorities are conducted at the highest level at the Center.

Other universities and colleges at Lincoln include Nebraska Wesleyan University, a Methodist institution, and Union College, sponsored by the Seventh Day Adventist denomination.

There are six colleges and universities in Omaha.

Edward and John Creighton came to Omaha in 1856 and gathered a large fortune through the operation of the Western Union Telegraph Company. In 1876 Mary Lucretia Creighton, widow of Edward, left $100,000 to found a school in memory of her husband. John A. Creighton over the years provided more than $2,000,000 for the institution which has become the widely known Creighton University. About a year after the school was founded, the Jesuits were given control. Other Omaha Catholic institutions include College of St. Mary, Duchesne College of Sacred Heart, and Servite College (two year). Grace Bible Institute at Omaha is independent. The city supports the Municipal University of Omaha, with an enrollment of nearly 6,000 students.

State institutions in addition to the University are Chadron State College, Kearney State College, Peru State College and Wayne State College. Other institutions of higher education in the state are Midland Lutheran College of Fremont, Concordia Teachers College, Seward, and Dana College, Blair—all Lutheran four-year colleges; Hastings

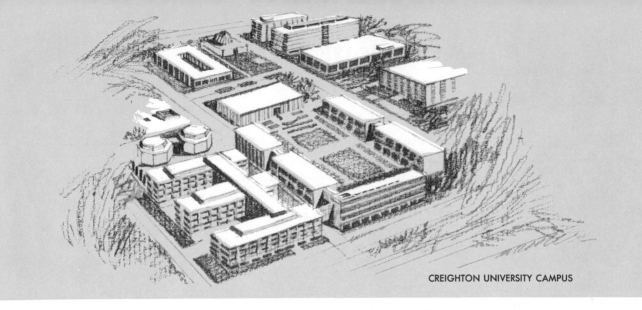

CREIGHTON UNIVERSITY CAMPUS

College is Presbyterian. Three new private colleges have appeared—John F. Kennedy College at Wahoo; John J. Pershing College at Beatrice; and the Hiram Scott College of Scottsbluff.

Two-year public junior colleges are at Fairbury, McCook, Norfolk, North Platte, Scottsbluff, and York.

Nebraska's first school was set up at Fort Atkinson in 1820. Missionaries soon established schools for the Indians. The first school for white children outside of the fort was begun at Bellevue in 1849. As time went by and the scattered population could afford to do so, schools were set up in various localities, most of them in the simplest kind of cabin or dugout. Parents of the pupils scraped together the meager salaries of the teachers.

The first legislature of the territory passed a law authorizing school districts administered by school boards which would provide free schools at the elementary level. Free high schools were not provided until 1875. Today Nebraska has about 2,600 public school districts enrolling close to 400,000 pupils. Private and parochial schools in the state enroll more than 60,000.

Collecting Your Thoughts

Will Nebraska schools and colleges be growing in the years ahead? See if you can find the estimates of how many pupils there will be in the public schools and in the colleges and universities ten years from today. What new problems will this bring to the schools?

Enchantment of Nebraska

Pathway to the Golden West

For more than a century the wide Platte Valley has been the high-road to the fabled lands of the setting sun. But for those who stayed and for those who come to visit today there is far more to Nebraska than a mere pathway, historic, glamorous and interesting as it is. Here is a land where the West that was wild continues to mingle with evidences of the most modern civilization.

Giant cattle herds still roam the unfenced prairies of a hundred years ago. But nuclear reactors power modern industry, and super-highways lace the green countryside, replacing the ruts of the Oregon Trail. Up-to-date cities have grown from the tracks of the Mormon wagons, and yet some of these are not out of hearing of Indian pow-wows and celebrations.

For the visitor there are the joys of farm and ranch vacations and many fine state parks, innumerable historical restorations and reproductions, fantastic scenery as well as some of the finest museums, music and other cultural attractions anywhere.

Home of a "Wonder"—Lincoln

"I came expecting to find a barren plain with possibly a few trees and modern buildings, and instead I found one of the architectural wonders of the world," wrote a foreign visitor to Lincoln. He was referring, of course, to the state capitol building, which architectural authority Linus Burr Smith declared was "world famous as an architectural triumph."

In 1948, 500 of the leading architects of the country were invited to take part in a poll to determine the 25 finest buildings the world has ever seen. When the results were made known, the Nebraska capitol was given fourth rank among all the buildings of the world's history.

Nebraska has had five capitol buildings—two territorial capitols in Omaha and three state capitols in Lincoln. The design for the present building was chosen in 1920 by a panel of jurors who considered the entries by number without knowing any of the architects' names. The winning design was the work of Bertram Grosvenor Goodhue.

According to Jane Tenhulzen, "Goodhue designed the beautiful

NEBRASKA CAPITOL AT LINCOLN

$10,000,000 State House as an expression of the Nebraska pioneer faith and frontier hope. Its tower rises as an exclamation point over a broad, firm base in daring defiance of the tradition that capitols should have pillars and domes. It stands as a crow's nest on a ship, surveying the rippling prairie, its golden tip symbolizing the inherent purpose of its citizens."

Ground was first broken for the building in 1922, and the new building was built around the old, which was still being used. Nebraska maintained its reputation for thrift by building the new capitol only as funds were available, so that when it was completed and dedicated in 1932 it was completely paid for even though it was finished in the heart of the depression and drought years.

At the time, the New York *Times* commented, "Either it will be a building of impressive force that will stretch its power milleniums in the future or it will be a stern-browed reminder of the money that could have been spent in better ways. Certainly, it will be no nonentity—no timid copy of dead art. Nebraska has been brave—has dared —where other states have bought their capitols more or less ready-to-wear, of the standardized Washington model."

The verdict of the years seems to be that of an unqualified and great success. The visitor today sees the massive building with the lofty limestone pinnacle of its tower ramming boldly against the prairie sky to a height of 400 feet—"a monument of the past and a promise of the future."

The symbolism of the carvings, murals, mosaics and other art is so complicated and the designs are so majestic the full meaning is difficult to grasp in only one visit. Gifts of Nature is the theme for the floor, walls, and ceiling of the vestibule. The construction of the mosaics required years of painstaking effort, cutting, fitting and placing. Miss Hildreth Meirie was the tile designer, and it is said she considered the capitol mosaics her greatest work.

The rotunda art, in the very heart of the 437-foot-square building, represents the creative energies. Dominating the rotunda floor is a giant mosaic of Ceres, goddess of agriculture. High above the floor is the dome of the rotunda, bearing the heroic figures of Charity, Faith, Courage, Temperance, Wisdom, Justice and Magnanimity. The viewer's eye is held by the great rotunda chandelier, the largest of its kind in the world, a huge bronze creation of 136 lights, suspended on a chain designed to hold 6,000 pounds. High above, the rotunda is encircled by 24 columns of the finest French marble, noted for its regular veining and soft glow. The rotunda balcony is guarded by a magnificently carved railing of onyx featuring sculptured meadowlark and buffalo.

The murals in the hall and the rotunda are the work of two artists. The homesteader's series was made by James Penney, with lavish use of reds, yellows, browns, buffs and other typical Nebraska colors. Inside the rotunda, the three heroic murals painted by Kenneth Evett represent the work of the head, hands and heart.

West of the great rotunda, lawmakers meet in the unicameral legislative chamber. Since Nebraska is the only state with a single legislative house, its capitol is the only one with a single legislative chamber.

Many of the capitol's interior rooms show especially beautiful workmanship and the loving care of artists and craftsmen. The ceiling in the Supreme Court is a remarkable example of this. The wood used is American walnut and there are nearly 8,000 separate pieces glued and pegged together, using no nails.

The outside of the capitol is made notable by many carvings, bas-reliefs, sculptures and inscriptions. One of the finest of these is a relief panel in the south balcony showing Franklin, Washington and other early leaders. Columns of the south entrance are topped by figures of lawmakers of ancient lands. Nebraska history is the theme of panels on the northeast corner. Heroic figures guard the lower bases of the tower. Most of the capitol stone relief work was done by Lee Lawrie.

Above all looms the gold-glazed tower, topped by the gigantic statue of the Sower—a symbolic figure "sowing the seeds of goodwill for a more noble living in the future." The statue is a bronze shell almost an inch thick, about 19 feet high on a base 13 feet high. Figure and base together weigh about nine tons.

It is estimated that if this extraordinary building could be duplicated today its cost would be $25,000,000—two and a half times its original cost.

Watching over the west steps is one of the nation's most impressive pieces of sculpture—the statue of Abraham Lincoln by Daniel Chester French, who did the Lincoln statue in the Lincoln Memorial at Washington. From the vantage point of the pedestal, the Civil War President appears to be brooding over the largest city to bear his name.

When the documents and furniture of the state government were moved from Omaha to Lincoln in 1868, there were only thirty people living in the new capital. The move was made at night to escape the armed bands of Omaha boosters who were determined to keep the capital by force if necessary. Only a year later the population had risen to 500 and by 1870 it had reached 2,500. Today Lincoln is Nebraska's second largest city.

Another of Lincoln's notable state buildings is the regal and elegant executive mansion, home of the governor, completed in 1957. Its striking rooms include the emerald state drawing room, enhanced by the elegance of hand-cut crystal chandeliers. Commuting is no problem for the governor since the mansion lies almost within the shadow of the capitol.

EXECUTIVE MANSION

An impressive lead in Lincoln's cultural affairs is provided by the University of Nebraska. The Nebraska State Museum is housed in Morrill Hall on the university campus. One of the most important exhibits is that of the world's largest mammoth, housed in Elephant Hall. Ralph Mueller Planetarium is also connected with the museum. Among the best-known landmarks on the campus is the great Memorial Stadium where many outstanding games have been played.

The university is also the home of one of the finest small art galleries in the country. The gallery was a gift of the Sheldon family in memory of Miss Mary Frances Sheldon and her brother, A. Bromley Sheldon, to provide the university with a building worthy of housing its extensive art collections. Jim Forrest has said "the gallery is both a building to house beauty and a thing of beauty in itself." Philip Johnson of New York was the architect, and he wrote, "Never have I known such joy in working out a problem . . . I am astonished at the artistic sophistication, at the direct, straightforward interest in the arts, so refreshing after the status-seeking snobbishness of many East Coast art lovers."

Another outstanding cultural institution housed at the university is the Nebraska State Historical Society.

Of the buildings owned by the city one of the most impressive is Pershing Municipal Auditorium. When the fully air-conditioned building was completed in 1957, the capital city at last had an auditorium with seating capacity of 7,000, the finest sound and lighting systems and a gigantic stage equipped with all the latest theater devices. In a matter of hours the auditorium becomes a boxing or wrestling arena, a roller skating rink, exhibition hall, circus arena and many other things. Over the main entrance is the largest ceramic mosaic tile mural ever undertaken in the United States; it shows the many activities possible inside.

Music lovers can depend on numbers of musical attractions both imported and local, highlighted by the Lincoln Symphony Orchestra.

The Lincoln home of William Jennings Bryan is open to the public as a registered National Historic Landmark. Here the national leader made his home until 1917. The first floor has been restored with the original furnishings and memorabilia of the Bryans.

A center of recreation for Lincoln is Antelope Park, with its zoo and famed children's zoo, considered one of the outstanding children's zoos in the nation. Also a delight for children is the Iron Horse Railroad, a scale replica of the famous C. P. Huntington locomotive. Hordes of happy young passengers ride around its half-mile track which winds along a creek, across a trestle and through a tunnel. Across from Antelope Park, visitors enjoy the majestic beauty of the Sunken Gardens.

Scene of many productions under the stars is scenic Pinewood Bowl, set deep in the heart of beautiful Pioneers Park.

Each spring Lincoln holds a Nebraskaland Parade, featuring among other attractions the reproduction of a pioneer conestoga wagon built for the Nebraska Game Commission. The wagon is pulled in parades and festivals all over the state by two Nebraska favorites, Neb and Raska, placid oxen trained to carry the heavy yoke and trundle the mighty wagon—symbol of Nebraska's pioneer days.

Doorman of the Western Gate—Omaha

On June 24, 1854, the Omaha Indians signed a treaty giving up their age-old homelands on which a great city, taking their name, was destined to grow. To celebrate, a group of people crossed the Missouri River on the ferry from Council Bluffs, Iowa, for a Fourth of July celebration and picnic on what is now Capitol Hill. A toast to Nebraska was offered, and Hadley D. Johnson replied with a "salute" from an anvil cannon. The hole in the top of the anvil was filled with powder, and a fuse put in. When the fuse was lighted, the anvil was flung a hundred feet into the air with a mighty roar. A group of Indians hurried over to see what had happened; women and children were frightened, and the party broke up in panic.

So Omaha history started with a bang; it continued that way; speculators, settlers, merchants and others who had been eagerly waiting the opening of the land hurried across the river to build a city. Streets 100-feet wide were staked out near the ferry landing opposite Council Bluffs, Iowa. Lots were sold for $25 each. In July, 1854, the first building in Omaha was constructed of logs at what is now the corner of Twelfth and Jackson streets. Soon the community had a hotel and restaurant, and by the end of the year there were 50 settlers.

Youthful Omaha had much of the slam-bang history of the frontier—gunfights, fortunes lost and made in gambling, and quick pioneer justice. The story is told that one rope was made to do the work of two when two men were lynched at the same time by throwing the rope over a tree and suspending a culprit from each end.

Justice and progress were not long in coming, although the first court case had "comic opera" overtones. The case was brought to court over the theft of half a cheese from Douglas House, one of the first hotels. An early account says, "The jury brought in a verdict of not guilty, at which the landlord flew into a rage and ordered the jury out of the house. This was a most serious situation, as there was no other place to stay. Finally, however, by the persuasion of friends and the return of the half cheese, the landlord relented, and thus ended the first lawsuit in Nebraska."

Soon steamboats were docking almost every day, bringing emigrants.

Ground was broken for the transcontinental railroad at Omaha in 1863. From that moment on, the future of Omaha as one of the country's great transportation and commercial metropolises was assured. Omaha took its place as doorman at the gateway to the West. Much of early Omaha history centers around its most enterprising families, such as the Creightons, Cudahys, Brandeis, Kountzes and Paxtons.

Nor does Omaha lack for energetic boosters today. One of the most unusual organizations anywhere is the Knights of Ak-Sar-Ben. The organization began in 1894 when a group of Omaha businessmen decided that some kind of an annual festival such as New Orleans' Mardi Gras would be good for their city. They hit on spelling Nebraska backward as the name of their organization. This annual Ak-Sar-Ben Ball and Coronation has become one of the country's best-known annual festivals. The organization sponsors sports events, livestock shows and rodeo, races and other events in its Ak-Sar-Ben Field and Coliseum. The Ak-Sar-Ben 4-H Baby Beef Show is said to be the most outstanding of its kind in the nation.

Another important gathering place is the mammoth Civic Auditorium, covering four city blocks. It includes an arena seating 10,000, a music hall with a 2,610 capacity, an assembly hall seating 600 and

OMAHA CIVIC AUDITORIUM

CREIGHTON
UNIVERSITY LIBRARY

BOYS TOWN

JOSLYN ART MUSEUM

MEDICAL
CENTER

UNIVERSITY OF OMAHA
ADMINISTRATION BUILDING

STRATEGIC AIR COMMAND HEADQUARTERS

an exhibition hall with 70,000 square feet of show space.

Pacing Omaha as a leading Midwest cultural center is the Joslyn Art Museum. This was donated by Mrs. George A. (Sarah) Joslyn in memory of her husband. The remarkable architecture of this $4,000,000 institution makes the building itself a work of art. More people visit and support the Joslyn Museum than any other art museum in the nation in proportion to population. Along with its many fine permanent collections, the museum offers such outstanding special exhibits as the display of the Dead Sea Scrolls in 1965.

Another principle cultural institution is the full-scale Omaha Symphony Orchestra.

An Omaha Medical Center has risen around the University of Nebraska College of Medicine. It includes a doctors' office building, the new Bishop Clarkson Memorial Hospital and Nursing School, and complete facilities for specialized treatment of children at Children's Memorial Hospital, one of the largest in the Midwest, served by 265 doctors. Special care is given to convalescent and handicapped children.

The City Emergency Hospital building was willed to the city by Anna Wilson, known as queen of the underworld. The city debated for some time about accepting the gift but finally considered that public service might sometimes arise from the least likely source.

Omaha is headquarters for the world's largest health and accident insurance company—Mutual of Omaha. As headquarters for 37 insurance companies, including the Woodmen of the World Life Insurance Company, Omaha has come to be known as the "Hartford of the West." Altogether there are 115 insurance company "home offices" in Omaha.

Offutt Air Force Base just south of Omaha is headquarters for the Strategic Air Command (SAC). SAC has been called "headquarters of the nation's peace-keeping force," and "nerve center for the global air defenses of the United States."

An entirely different kind of institution, yet equally well-known, is Boys Town near Omaha. It has been called "A thrilling American success story whose fame has spread across the world." Started by Father Edward J. Flanagan, its renown was spread when the movie *Boys Town* was made, starring Mickey Rooney and Spencer Tracy.

Another Omaha activity in which young men play a leading role is what is known as the "College World Series." This is the championship baseball play-off of the National Collegiate Athletic Association.

Some poignant memories of the pioneer past may still be aroused in modern Omaha. There is the Mormon Cemetery, site of one of the Mormons' winter camps in the region. When the winter took the lives of 600 of the Saints, they were buried there. One of the most unusual and touching of monuments is the statue of a Mormon father and mother standing mute and dejected over the open grave of their dead child.

A well-known collection of Americana is contained in the Museum of the Union Pacific Railroad. Here are many relics of the railroad's history. There is a fine display of Lincoln material, including a replica of his funeral railroad coach.

The city is well represented with gardens and parks. Mount Vernon Gardens is a replica of those on the estate of George Washington. They overlook the Missouri River basin site passed by Lewis and Clark in 1804. Riverview Park, with its zoo, is another popular feature. Levi Carter Park now rests on a piece of Iowa which was cut off by the Missouri River and left in Omaha in 1877. Just a few miles from the heart of Omaha is Fontenelle Forest, largest tract of virgin timber in Nebraska. This wilderness area has been recognized by the Federal government as one of the top seven natural history sites in the nation.

The Rest of the East

"Nestled in the rolling hills above the Missouri River, Brownville is a living embodiment of the past," according to *Nebraskaland* magazine. "Untouched by the dash and turmoil of today, Brownville retains the restful atmosphere and quiet charm of nineteenth century America. Its drowsy Main Street, dusty side roads, and steamboat architecture have survived today's mad rush."

To enhance Brownville as a tourist attraction, the Historical Society has restored several old mansions, and others will be opened in the future. The Carson House is equipped with post-Civil War furnishings; the Muir house, Furnas home, and Captain Bailey's house, now a free museum, and the grist mill are other attractions.

Each year Brownville holds a festival to celebrate old times. The

74

people dress in period costumes. There are horse-drawn buggies. A flea market is held on Main Street and candle making, rug weaving and flax spinning are demonstrated.

Another aspect of history is remembered at Beatrice. Here is the unique Homestead National Monument of America. The land of Daniel Freeman, who claimed to be the nation's first homesteader, was set aside in 1936 through the efforts of Senator George W. Norris and others as "a proper memorial emblematical of the hardships and the pioneer life through which the early settlers passed in the settlement." There is a visitor center, and the Palmer-Epard homestead cabin has been moved there with furnishings and tools as used by the pioneers.

Each year Beatrice celebrates Homestead Week in June. The trial of Wild Bill Hickok which followed the McCanless showdown at nearby Rock Creek Pony Express station is recreated in rip-roaring fun. Top cowboys vie for heavy purses at the rodeo, and there are parades, carnivals and beard contests.

Nearby Fairbury celebrates every August with its "Echoes of the Oregon Trail" pageant, featuring a cast of 200, which brings to life many of the storied characters of the region, and also recreates the Hickok-McCanless affair.

BROWNVILLE FESTIVAL

Another historical pageant is that honoring Princess Alice Blue Cloud, daughter of Red Cloud. The Princess died and was buried on a bluff of the Republican River looking down over the city that bears her father's name. Her favorite pony was buried beside her. Each year on the Fourth of July the community recreates the events of the princess' life and the passing of the Indian era. Chief Red Cloud was the last great warrior chief of the Ogallala Sioux. He held two important war councils on the site of the city that bears his name.

Red Cloud also remembers its most famous daughter, the authoress Willa Cather. Willa Cather Museum is housed in one of the town's original buildings.

Another museum, unusual for a community of its size, is Hastings' House of Yesterday. The museum features the "world's largest collection on the rare whooping crane," historical Nebraska articles and agricultural implements, old-time fashions, and 35 habitat groups, along with many other exhibits. Also available is the J. M. McDonald Foundation Planetarium, gift of the foundation to the city. In 1877 Hastings won election as county seat. However, it was denied this honor until a group of Hastings citizens stole into rival Juniata, put the county records on lumber wagons and scurried back with them to Hastings.

Near Minden is Pioneer Village, 22 buildings housing a collection of more than 30,000 items of pioneer Nebraska. A hundred antique autos, horse-drawn vehicles, and the world's largest collection of farm tractors may be seen there. The buildings include an original sod house, Pony Express station, and old schoolhouse.

Fort Kearney was moved to present Kearney in 1848 to protect the Oregon Trail. This important outpost is being restored as Fort Kearney Historical Park, and much of it may now be seen by visitors. Because of its central location in the United States, Kearney at one time had hoped of becoming capital of the United States.

According to Arnie Garson, "One of the most magnificent commercial and cultural centers of its days was located at Kearney." This was the $150,000 Kearney Opera House, the only place between the Missouri River and Denver with a stage large enough for major productions.

Grand Island was founded by a group of Davenport, Iowa, men who also had the hope that it might someday become the national capital.

The city did not achieve this goal, but it did manage to become the third largest city in Nebraska.

Leo Stuhr, son of a pioneer Grand Island family, contributed 115 acres of land and $500,000 to create the Stuhr Museum and its surrounding Land of the Prairie Pioneer. Famed American architect Edward Durell Stone designed the museum building to rest on an island in a man-made lake. On Pioneer Prairie a trail will take the visitor past a re-created Pawnee Village, an old Grand Island settlement, a nineteenth century farm, and a turn-of-the-century village with both business and residential districts. Additional features are an agricultural demonstration area, a botanical garden and an outdoor amphitheater.

One of the principal buildings of Grand Island is handsome and imposing Grand Island Roman Catholic Cathedral.

Near Grand Island is Stoley State Park. Here in 1864 William Stoley built a kind of private fortress which he called Fort Independence to protect his family and nearby settlers from the Indians. The fort boasted an underground stable 88 feet long.

Comparatively few of the Indians who once troubled the Stoleys and others now remain in Nebraska. Winnebago is a small Indian town, headquarters of the Winnebago Indian Agency.

At Bancroft the life and work of Nebraska poet laureate John G. Neihardt are remembered in the quaint little one-room cabin that he used for a study. The room is filled with manuscripts, first editions and other mementoes of the world-famed poet. On the grounds is a Sioux prayer garden such as the one he described in *Black Elk Speaks*.

Fremont was named for General John C. Frémont. Its municipal auditorium, seating 3,500, is unusual for a city of its size.

One of Nebraska's best-known estates is at Nebraska City. This is the former home of J. Sterling Morton, Arbor Lodge. The 52-room Morton mansion was given to the state by the family and is now a part of Arbor Lodge State Historical Park. Here each year the founder of Arbor Day is honored on his birthday, April 22, with a tree-planting ceremony. Another Nebraska City landmark is John Brown's cave, a major station on the underground railroad. It was conducted by famed abolitionist John Brown. The first high school building in Nebraska was built at Nebraska City in 1864.

Western Nebraska

"Hewitt in his dugout,/ Sought a name for his P.O./ He suggested several/ But Uncle Sam said 'No.'/ His two boys went a hunting/ An Indian bow brought back./ 'Twas broken, but they hung it/ Upon the dugout shack./ He shouted when he saw it,/ 'This name will surely go.'/ And Uncle Sam okayed it—/ That's why it's 'Broken Bow.'"

This doggerel verse may not be exactly accurate, but it is a fact that one of the most unique town names in the country came into being when Wilson Hewitt found a broken Indian bow. At Broken Bow is the only two-story sod house still standing in the United States.

Broken Bow is the eastern gateway to the vast Nebraska Sandhills region. As George A. Peterson said in *Prairie Paradox*, "There is no other geographic spot like it in the world—20 counties of north-central Nebraska—where lush green grasses now cover once-naked, wind-blown dunes of desert sand; where a land of taboo has become a land of plenty. . . . Hard-bitten soldiers and cowboys feared a land they believed to be without water, and they swapped tales of people who had gone in but never come out. . . .

"Not until 1879 did E. S. Newman, whose ranch stretched from the Niobrara at Valentine west to Wyoming, start using the lake country. Even then it was by accident. It was, in fact, out of sheer desperation that an attempt was made to rescue a few of the 6,000 head of cattle stampeded by a March blizzard into the mysterious Hills.

"In April after the snow had melted, 12 courageous men rode into the interior. After five weeks of roundup they brought out 3,000 more cattle that had drifted in . . . —9,000 beeves . . . fatter and sleeker than those at the home ranch." From that time on Sandhills became a favorite of cattlemen.

At Valentine is Sawyers' Sandhills Museum, where exhibits tell much of the romance of the region. Near Valentine is Fort Niobrara National Wildlife Refuge, which has a museum of natural history of the region. A now rare prairie-dog town is preserved there. Visitors are fascinated by the roundup twice each year of the picturesque buffalo herd, numbering more than 200. Once again the prairie thunders to thudding hooves. The calves are tagged, branded and turned loose to roam. An-

other rare sight on the refuge is the herd of 150 Texas longhorns.

A natural spectacle near Valentine is Snake River Falls.

Rushville still remembers the visit of Calvin Coolidge while he was President. One of the most popular pictures of the President was taken near Rushville. This was the one so often published showing Coolidge in an enormous cowboy hat.

During the 1860's James Bordeaux operated a fur trading post at Chadron. His post has been completely restored on the original foundations, as the Museum of the Fur Trade. In this unique display great effort has been made to present the story of trapping as Bordeaux and other rugged mountain men knew it. The museum features one of the finest collections of Northwest Indian trade guns found anywhere.

Chadron State Park is the largest state park in Nebraska.

SNAKE RIVER FALLS

The name of Crow Butte near Whitney recalls a poignant tale of the Crow braves who took refuge on the butte. Their Sioux enemies besieged the rock. However, the Crow cut apart their blankets, tied them together, and the young men escaped down the unguarded steep side. To keep the Sioux from becoming suspicious, the old men of the Crow danced and sang noisily all night. When the Sioux discovered they had been tricked, they let the old men go because they thought they were ordered to do so by messages in the white clouds floating over the butte. Soon they made a long-term peace with the Crow.

At Crawford, the historic fort founded in 1874 in the midst of the Indian troubles has become Fort Robinson State Park, with a museum of natural history and history. North of Crawford are the Nebraska badlands, not so well known as those of the Dakotas but having a grotesque, wild beauty all their own. A part of this wild and fantastic region has been set aside as Toadstool Park, where the gnarled landscape casts an enchanting spell.

The fossil beds near Agate have been proposed as Agate Fossil Beds National Monument, and only the action of Congress and the President is required to preserve this extraordinary national treasure.

In the Alliance Cemetery are the graves of Jules Sandoz and his wife. Sandoz, the vibrant horticulturist of the Sandhills, is memorialized in his daughter's *Old Jules*.

Scottsbluff was named for Hiram Scott, a fur trader who died in the region in 1828. His death is described by Washington Irving in his *Adventures of Captain Bonneville:* ". . . Scott was taken ill; and his companions came to a halt, until he should recover health and strength sufficient to proceed. While they were searching round in quest of edible roots, they discovered a fresh trail of white men, who had evidently recently preceded them. What was to be done? By a forced march they might overtake this party, and thus be able to reach the settlements in safety.

"Should they linger they might all perish of famine and exhaustion. Scott, however, was incapable of moving; they were too feeble to aid him forward, and dreaded that such a clog would prevent their coming up with the advance party. They determined, therefore, to abandon him to his fate. Accordingly, under pretense of seeking food . . . they deserted him and hastened forward upon the trail. They succeeded in overtaking the party of which they were in quest, but concealed their faithless desertion of Scott, alleging that he had died of disease.

"On the ensuing summer, the very individuals visiting these parts in company with others, came suddenly upon the bleached bones and grinning skull of a human skeleton, which, by certain signs they recognized for the remains of Scott. This was sixty long miles from the place where they had abandoned him; and it appeared that the wretched man had crawled that immense distance before death put an end to his miseries."

The 800 foot bluff at Scottsbluff has now become Scotts Bluff National Monument, with a museum of relics of pioneers of the region.

When railroad surveyors came upon the wagon wheel marking the grave of Rebecca Winters, a Mormon woman who died there on the trail, they changed their survey so the railroad would go around the grave, and they had a fence built around the spot. Later they discovered that Mrs. Winters' son was still living. A granite marker now guards the spot as a memorial to all mothers who died on the trail.

One of the most famed landmarks of the trail was spiked Chimney Rock between Gering and Bayard. It thrusts its peak 350 feet above the Platte River like the spike on a German helmet of World War I.

Sidney, Big Springs, and Ogallala were among the "rip-roaring" towns of Western history. Twenty-three saloons once crowded a single

block of Sidney, where the saloons, dance halls and gambling houses never closed. Shootings were so common they caused almost no attention. At a dance one night someone was shot; the corpse was propped up in the corner; the dancing went on; a second corpse joined the first; only after a third corpse joined the other two did the party come to an end. Today Sidney is a peaceful farm trading center.

At the end of the cattle trail, Ogallala "roared loudly enough to

83

provide a decade of scripts for television westerns." As one historian reported, "Gold flowed freely across the tables, liquor across the bar, and occasionally blood across the floor as a smoking gun in the hands of a jealous rival or an angered gambler brought an end to the trail of some unfortunate cowhand on the stained boards of 'Tuck's' Saloon.... Its gaming tables were never empty, its bar never dry, and its ladies never too preoccupied but what the newly-arrived cowhand found a welcome."

According to George Peterson, "Ogallala residents knew on sight the faces of some of the west's most notorious gunmen. One was Doc (Daniel C.) Middleton, Nebraska's most infamous outlaw. Whether he deserved it or not, he got credit for all the livestock stealing crimes within 500 miles of his Sandhills hideout. Another was professional gambler Luke Short, whose name was made the day he outdrew Jim Courtright, Texas' famed quick-shot artist."

Many of the frontier characters are buried in the Boot Hill Cemetery of Ogallala. Today at Ogallala some of the frontier past may be relived in the reproduction of Front Street, where shoot-outs are staged for visitors even more regularly than the real thing occurred.

At Arthur, 34 miles north of Ogallala, is Pilgrim Holiness Church, built in 1928 out of baled hay. Another interesting church was the one at Keystone, with a Catholic altar at one end and the other end arranged for Protestant services. The most unusual feature was the reversible pews which let the different congregations face the altar of their faith.

No one had ever robbed a Union Pacific train until notorious outlaw Sam Bass and his gang stopped one at Big Springs station. They greedily helped themselves to three crates of gold pieces—an unexpected stroke of luck. The passengers were lined up and made to give up their valuables. When Sam saw one man had only one arm he gave back his watch and money. A Texas cattleman stashed his $3,100 under a chair and Don Fretwell palmed his big diamond in his boot, but Sam and his gang pocketed $1,300 in addition to the gold.

Near Lewellen was one of the most heartbreaking points on the western trails. This was Windlass Hill, a terribly steep route from the bluff top to the river bottom. An English traveler in 1849 wrote that

"no one spoke for two miles, the descent was so breath-taking. . . . Riders dismounted and led their horses, wagon wheels were locked and the wagons steadied with ropes." There were many casualties of men and beasts as well as equipment.

The Memorial Art Gallery at Chappel is noteworthy in a town of its size, especially for its fine collection of etchings by such artists as Rembrandt and Whistler. Another small community with an extraordinary public facility is Gothenburg, where the community building seats 3,600.

McCook is noted as a meat-packing center. It bears the name of General Alexander McDowell McCook. It was the home of Senator George W. Norris.

Near Maxwell is Fort McPherson Military Cemetery. Bodies were brought here from more than twenty military posts of the West after the Indian wars ceased. Buffalo Bill was once stationed here as a scout.

North Platte is the metropolis of central and western Nebraska. Here the north and south branches come together to form the Platte River. For thirty years North Platte was home to famed frontier showman Buffalo Bill. In 1882, Buffalo Bill put on a Fourth of July celebration. This was such a success that he was inspired to bring together a large number of trick riders, sharpshooters and other experts in the lore of the West. After much practice with this group he created the wild west show for which he later gained world fame. That first Fourth of July show is claimed to be the world's first rodeo, although that is disputed by Texas. Each year North Platte stages its Buffalo Bill Blowout in honor of the showman.

Buffalo Bill's Scouts Rest Ranch at North Platte is open to the public. In the gigantic barn where his wild west acts trained, are yellowing posters acclaiming the show. The rafter supports have been carved into the shape of gun stocks. The 19-room mansion may be viewed by visitors, and there is a museum of period furniture and Buffalo Bill mementoes.

In Memorial Park is another museum, the D. A. R. Museum, a small cedar cabin. Here are early utensils, relics from Custer's last stand and other reminders of the early west—the proud heritage on which Nebraska has built such a varied present.

"BUFFALO BILL" CODY

Handy Reference Section

Instant Facts

Became the 37th state March 1, 1867
Capital—Lincoln, settled 1856
State Motto—*Equality Before the Law*
Familiar Name—Cornhusker State
State Bird—Western Meadowlark
State Tree—American Elm
State Flower—Goldenrod
Area—77,407 square miles
Greatest Length (north to south)—210 miles
Greatest Width (east to west)—430 miles
Highest Point—5,430 feet, western Banner County
Lowest Point—825 feet, southeast corner Richardson County
Geographic Center—Custer, 10 miles northwest of Broken Bow
Highest Recorded Temperature—118° (Minden)
Lowest Recorded Temperature—minus 47° (Camp Clarke)
Population—1,540,000 (1966 estimate)
Population Density—18.4 persons per square mile (1960 census)

Principal Cities—Omaha	345,000	(1965 estimate)
Lincoln	128,521	(1960 census)
Grand Island	25,742	
Hastings	21,412	
Fremont	19,698	

You Have a Date with History

1541—Coronado crosses Nebraska plains
1598—Onate enters region
1682—French claim entire western region
1720—Pedro de Villasur killed by Indians
1738—Mallet brothers visit Nebraska
1804—Nebraska region becomes American; Lewis and Clark explore
1806—Pike explores
1811—Wilson Price Hunt crosses state
1812—Fort Lisa established
1819—Stephen Long expedition marks Nebraska as "desert"
1823—Bellevue begun, becomes first permanent settlement

1833—First Nebraska mission
1842—John C. Frémont crosses Nebraska
1847—Mormon trek begins
1849—49ers cross Nebraska on way to California
1854—Nebraska becomes a territory
1863—Daniel Freeman claims first homestead
1867—Statehood; railroad completed across Nebraska
1871—University of Nebraska opens
1887—William Jennings Bryan comes to Nebraska
1898—Trans-Mississippi Exposition, Omaha
1902—Nebraska National Forest established
1904—Kincaid law permits 640 acre homesteads
1917—World War I begins, in which 47,801 Nebraskans serve
1932—Capitol dedicated
1934—Nebraska becomes only unicameral state
1941—World War II begins, in which 120,000 Nebraskans serve
1957—Governors Mansion completed; new Omaha charter
1963—Nation's first sodium graphite reactor opens near Lincoln

Thinkers, Doers, Fighters

People of renown who have been associated with Nebraska

Aldrich, Bess Streeter
Astaire, Fred
Beadle, George W.
Bessey, Charles
Blackbird (Chief)
Brando, Marlon
Bryan, William Jennings
Cather, Willa
Cody, William F. (Buffalo Bill)
Cook, James H.
Creighton, Edward
Creighton, John
Dawes, Charles G.
Flanagan, Edward J.
Fonda, Henry

Hanson, Howard
Houston, James (Jim)
Joslyn, George A.
Judd, Walter
Lloyd, Harold
Morton, J. Sterling
Neihardt, John Gneisenau
Norris, George William
Piper, Edwin Ford
Sandoz, Jules
Sandoz, Mari
Sheldon, A. Bromley
Stuhr, Leo
Taylor, Robert

Annual Events

April—Arbor Day, Nebraska City
April—Five-State Art Show, Scottsbluff
April—1884 Days Celebration, Valentine
June—Homesteaders Days, Beatrice
June—College Baseball World Series, Omaha
June—Old Timers Day, Osceola
June—Nebraskaland Days, Lincoln
June—Harvest Celebration, Laurel
July—Princess Alice Blue Cloud Pageant, Red Cloud
July—Alice Blue Cloud Pageant, Crystal Lake
July—Oregon Trail Days, Gering
July—Black Powder Shoot and Parade, Holbrook
July-August—Indian Pow-Wow, Winnebago
August—Echoes of the Oregon Trail Pageant, Fairbury
August—Omaha Indian Pow-Wow Council, Macy
August—Buffalo Bill Blowout, North Platte
August—Nebraska Czech Festival, Wilber
August—Hay Days Celebration, Atkinson
September—Hay Days Celebration, Cozad
September—State Fair, Lincoln
September—Old Home Town Festival, Brainerd
October—Ak-Sar-Ben, Omaha
October—World's Championship Rodeo, Omaha
December—"Christmas Island Lighting Night," Grand Island

OLD-FASHIONED BLACK POWDER SHOOT

INDEX

92

93

About the Author: Allan Carpenter was born in Waterloo, Iowa. He went to Iowa State College and then taught at a Des Moines Junior High School and at Drake University. He left teaching to found the magazine TEACHERS' DIGEST which he published for eight years. He has been associated with publishing for many years and now works full time as a free-lance writer. His first book was published when he was 20 and since then he has written over fifty books.

———

About the Illustrator: Roger Herrington grew up in Sault Ste. Marie, Michigan, on the American side of the Soo Locks. His stepfather was a tugboat captain which took the family to many parts of the United States. While he was in college, Roger worked during summers as a boatman on the Erie Canal. He went to the American Academy of Art in Chieago for his art training, and spent two years at the Ringling School of Art in Sarasota, Florida. He now has his own studio in Chicago and devotes most of his working time to illustrating books.